Ouida

Syrlin

Vol. 3

Ouida

Syrlin
Vol. 3

ISBN/EAN: 9783337293307

Printed in Europe, USA, Canada, Australia, Japan

Cover: Foto ©Thomas Meinert / pixelio.de

More available books at **www.hansebooks.com**

SYRLIN

VOL. III.

NEW NOVELS AT ALL LIBRARIES.

WITHOUT LOVE OR LICENCE: a Tale of South Devon. By HAWLEY SMART. Second Edition. 3 vols.

BLIND LOVE. By WILKIE COLLINS. With a Preface by WALTER BESANT. Second Edition. 3 vols.

FOR THE LOVE OF A LASS. By AUSTIN CLARE. 2 vols.

AN OCEAN TRAGEDY. By W. CLARK RUSSELL. 3 vols.

A LAST LOVE. By GEORGES OHNET. 1 vol.

A NOBLE WOMAN. By HENRY GREVILLE. 1 vol.

THE DEAD MAN'S SECRET. By J. E. MUDDOCK. 1 vol.

THE HOLY ROSE, &c. By WALTER BESANT. 1 vol.

PAUL JONES'S ALIAS, &c. By D. CHRISTIE MURRAY and HENRY HERMAN. 1 vol.

THE LAWTON GIRL. By HAROLD FREDERIC. 1 vol.

London: CHATTO & WINDUS, 214 Piccadilly, W.

BY

OUIDA

'The World is too much with us'

IN THREE VOLUMES

VOL. III.

London
CHATTO & WINDUS, PICCADILLY
1890

PRINTED BY
SPOTTISWOODE AND CO., NEW-STREET SQUARE
LONDON

SYRLIN

CHAPTER XXXVIII

'IF she thinks that I am satisfied she will become incautious,' Avillion said to himself, with that ingenuity of reasoning which many intrigues had taught him. His feeling against his wife was very bitter; wounded vanity is crueller than any jealousy into which love has entered; the latter may relent, the former will never pardon. But the effect produced on her was wholly opposite to that which he anticipated. Having, as she imagined, been trusted by him, and having found in him, as she fancied, a generous and chivalrous sentiment, she was angered against herself, and disposed to a still greater irritation against Syrlin. Like most women her feelings moved *per saltum*, and were apt to move in the contrary direction to the one pointed out or permitted. All the stimulus which prohibition, irritation, and injustice had given, suddenly sank to nothing under the entire liberty and approval which she believed that Avillion accorded her. Conscience makes cowards of the proudest, and for the first time in her life her conscience was uneasy. Under the spur of it she did what he was far from expecting. She left London for Aix-les-Bains, accompanying her sister, Lady Ilfracombe, whose health was delicate. People were going to Aix every day; it was the middle of July, and there was nothing singular in her departure. Yet, as it was unannounced, Flodden stared helplessly in the porter's face when, at the gates of Avillion House, that functionary said blandly:

'Her ladyship left for Haix by tidal train this morning, my lord. No, we don't know anything as to how long, we have no horders; his lordship's in town still.'

Flodden moved from the gates and went down Piccadilly with the stunned sensation of a person who has fallen from a high cliff in the course of a summer day's stroll. Aix was indeed a mere succursale of London; easy of access, and at that moment filled with English invalids of his acquaintance; but the knowledge that she had gone out of England without as much as even a word to him of her intention, brought home to him suddenly and intensely the fact that he was nothing in her life; merely one of the innumerable young men whose name was on her visiting-list, who had not and never could have on her any claim except for cards to her parties and a kind word or two from her lips in the crowds of society.

As he passed the St. James's Hotel he ran against a man who was coming away from it, and, hurriedly apologising, as he did so he recognised Syrlin.

'She is gone away!' said Flodden almost unconsciously; his blue eyes had a dazed strained expression in them as they looked upward at his brilliant rival.

'Since when is it permitted to speak of a lady without her name?' said Syrlin rudely and haughtily, as, without asking who was intended by the pronoun, he pushed Flodden towards the curbstone and went on his way through the streams of people passing to and fro towards Hyde Park Corner.

'It is no news to him,' thought the boy with a jealous misery, in which all consciousness of the affront done to himself was drowned. Syrlin had become acquainted with her departure only half-an-hour earlier than himself, and in the same manner, at the gates of her house; but it did not pain or bewilder him; he understood her motives by intuition, and he merely said to his servant, 'I go to Paris this evening.'

With her away from it, London could not hold him a day.

Flodden went through the dusty mist which obscures Piccadilly on a July afternoon, and looked down over the confused jumble of horses' heads, carriage liveries, omnibus roofs, waggon loads, men's hats, women's bonnets, servants' cockades, opened parasols, and flourished whips which filled to repletion that narrow and popular thoroughfare at such an hour. The trees looked jaded and powdered with dust like the pedestrians; the balcony flowers were a glare of blue lobelia, yellow calceolaria, scarlet geranium; the cab horses and the carriage horses were alike sweating and flinging up in the air their poor curb-worried jaws; here and there a muzzled dog went sadly with drooped head and tail, and heaving flanks; the basket women held out in vain roses which the noon-heat had blanched, and carnations out of which the heavy heat had sucked the sweetness.

The ladies in the carriages, like the flowers, were languid and pale from the late hours, the hurried pleasures, the too numerous engagements, of the waning season.

It was an epitome of London, with its sharp and cruel contrasts, its oppressive stress, and strain, and din, and crush, its immense wealth, its frightful poverty, its utter and irremediable failure to make civilisation endurable, riches excusable, or luxury beautiful, which was here before him in the choked channel of this narrow street; the boy felt as if the yellow dust, the lurid mist of it, suffocated him.

'Buy a buttonhole, my pretty gentleman,' whined a poor woman, standing at the corner of Dover Street with little bunches of rosebuds in her basket; little moss-rosebuds chiefly, homely, pleasant things, smelling of the country-side and the garden hedge, mates for the lark's song, and the bee's hum, and the cricket's chirp, when the day is high. 'Buy a buttonhole!' she repeated, holding up the drooping thirsty buds. 'I went all the way to Barnet for 'em, and I han't sold one.'

It was the professional beggar's whine: no doubt the professional beggar's lie; but verses of Lytton's 'Misery,' of Rossetti's 'Jenny,' rose to Flodden's mind in that lingering influence of verse which makes the poet more potent than the preacher in his generation.

A constable who knew Flodden pushed the girl roughly aside, and threatened her.

'As God lives it's gospel truth,' she cried in shrill despair. 'I han't had bit nor sup to-day, and th' old woman's dyin'. Come and see if you don't believe—'

'They all tell these tales, my lord,' said the policeman slightingly. 'I'll run her in if she go on molesting.'

'She has done no harm: she only wants to sell her rosebuds,' said Flodden; and then turning to the girl, he said gently, 'I will come with you and see if it be as bad as you say.'

And gravely, without any consciousness that he was doing an unheard of and supremely ridiculous thing, he put a half-sovereign in her hand, and bade her show him where she lived.

'But you won't walk with the likes o' me?' she said, breathless and gaping.

'Why not?' said the lad, dreamily, and despite the protests, entreaties, and ejaculations of the constable he persisted in bidding her lead the way to her dwelling-place.

'She'll get you in a slum, and have you

hocussed or murdered for your swag, sir,' muttered the guardian of law and order, vainly imploring attention.

'I do not think so,' said Flodden, with the obstinacy of a gentle temper; and he took her by the hand. 'Take me to your home,' he repeated; and the throngs in the streets beheld with wonder a youth of aristocratic appearance, and wearing the clothes of civilisation, pacing calmly by the side of a tatterdemalion with ragged skirts and rough uncombed locks, who carried a dirty basket half full of dead and dying rosebuds.

'If he warn't a peer he'd be clapped in Bedlam,' said the constable, with scorn, to a comrade. 'Them swells thinks to do the Shaftesbury dodge, and curry favour with the roughs that way; but it's all rot, says I, and won't do 'em a mossel o' good: the people hates 'em.'

He looked with deep disgust after the disappearing forms of Flodden and the girl, whom some boys were following with gibes and gestures and antics, while a passing cabman smacked his whip and holloaed out, 'Go it, old gal, you've got a bloomin' fancy man!'

'You shouldn't be seed with the likes o'

me, sir,' said the woman. 'It'll hurt you with your friends if you're seed with the likes o' me.'

'I have no friends,' said Flodden. It seemed to him that he had none: no one really cared! Would anyone even tell him the truth?

The girl perceived, with her town-sharpened senses, the ludicrous incongruity and impropriety of this young gentleman walking by her side in the streets of London; but Flodden did not see it, nor would he have cared if he had.

'Tell me your history,' he said to her, disregarding the jeers and shouts of the boys dancing about them. She complied: telling it with the useless repetition, the bald common wording, the involved and confused phrases of the poor, whose vocabulary is as meagre as their cupboard is empty. It was an ordinary story, of a family which had left its village thinking to better itself in the great wilderness of London; of the ravages made by fever and by smallpox amongst them; of the difficulty of finding work for the survivors, of the gradual melancholy slipping downward from respectable well-to-do industry to enforced inaction, indigence, and hunger.

'O! all nine o' us there's only me and mother left,' she said in conclusion. 'And she aren't long for this world, she's that bad. I han't ate anything for a good whiles, but I'm strong I am ; mother's racked wi' cough and rheumatis, and she can't stand up against it. If you don't mind, sir, I'll stop at a shop and buy some bread and tea with this here money as you've gived me?'

'Of course; good heavens! how could I forget,' said Flodden, contrite and heart-stricken ; it is so difficult to realise that there are actually people close at hand to you who want food. The young woman would not stay to eat anywhere herself, but she bought some bread and other things and laid them away beside the dead roses. She had nothing romantic, picturesque, or interesting about her ; she had the short broad features, the wide mouth, and the small pale eyes of the common English type; but the face was honest, and the regard was clear and wistful.

'She is telling me the truth,' thought Flodden, and he would have carried the bread and the tea for her if she would have allowed him.

Her miserable home lay Westminster way, and as they went to it, many men who knew

Flodden passed them in the streets about the Houses of Parliament.

'The young ass!' said one of them, echoing the sentiments of the constable. 'He ought to be put in a strait-waistcoat. That is Lorraine Iona's doing; he makes all those boys as mad as hatters.'

'Yes, it is very odd,' said another, who was of a more meditative turn. 'The Encyclopédistes first set those philanthropic bubbles floating, and the result was the Terror. One would think this generation might take warning, but it doesn't.'

'You cannot quench revolutions with rose-water,' said a third, 'and England is in revolution every whit as much as it was in Charles's time; only it creeps like a slow match, and its Declaration of Right disguises itself under Local Government Bills, and Allotment Bills, and Leaseholders Bills, and Liability of Owners Bills, and all the rest of the small fry which are eating away the constitution and the capital of the country.'

'What is to be done?' said the second speaker. 'The people will have these Bills, or something like them.'

'It's the d——d philanthropists who put it into their heads,' said the first speaker.

'It is the d——d manufacturers who create the cause of it,' said the other. 'If a revolution were sure to put an end to manufacturers, I would not quarrel with it.'

'Railway directors are as bad as manufacturers.'

'And brewers worse than either!'

'Oh-ho! And Maltby's peerage?'

'Maltby's peerage makes one agree with William Morris, that there is no longer an aristocracy in Great Britain. Nothing is odder than the fact that in England the very nature and meaning of a nobility has been forgotten, for nobility has been completely smothered under wealth; the once proud heart has lost its power to beat beneath the rolls of fat which have grown up around it.'

Meantime, while his critics thus disputed, Flodden went steadily on his way to the wretched tenements which lie south of Westminster, where undaunted he accompanied his companion to her home, and found her tale true in every respect.

The sights, the sounds, the smells, the ghastly needs and woes which he saw and heard of there, where she made her wretched home which yet was dear to her, brought close to him the gigantic and awful meaning of that squalid poverty with which the philanthropy of the drawing-rooms and of the newspapers plays and postures, as a baby might toy with a boa-constrictor.

It increased and intensified the depression of spirit which was already upon him, but it suited him better than the gossip of the clubs and the frivolity of garden-parties would have done.

The girl was penniless, ignorant, very common, yet she belonged to the class of respectable poor, who even in their deepest depths keep out of vice and cling to honesty, rather from instinct than from deliberate choice. But misery had brought her into one of the most wretched quarters of London, and the house in which she and her mother rented the corner of one damp, raw, naked chamber, shared with others as unhappy as themselves, was the embodiment of that squalid and hideous form of want which London creates and contains in a more absolutely horrible shape than any other city of Europe.

He passed the rest of the day there, careless of any personal danger which he might run from infection or from robbery, and absorbed in the spectacle of this sordid, grovelling, utterly hopeless aggregation of woes.

What a dreadful insanity it is which brings all these poor people from their villages to crowd and starve and perish in the dens of London! he thought. Poverty must be dreadful anywhere, but it must surely be less terrible where the fresh wind blows over the turnip fields or the clover crops than cooped up thus between sooty brick walls without a breath of air!

And he asked her if she would not like to go back to her deserted hamlet on the Berkshire Downs.

'Sure it was main and sweet there,' she answered, ' and for iver so long, sir, whenever I passed a barrow o' greens and sniffed the cabbages and lettuces that smelt so homelike, I did feel a lump in my throat, and such whiles I'd even thoughts o' settin' off to go back on foot, I was that hungry for the smell o' the soil. But now I donno; I got used to this rattle and row; it's lifelike as 'twere, and I can't say as I wouldn't be dull among the old meadows at home.'

Dull! Merciful powers! thought Flodden; dull! this poor wretch dragging her sore feet over the flags with her empty bowels yearning within her could talk of the peaceful heaven of country silence and country freshness as 'dull!'—could find in the hell of the streets where she starved unheeded, the same stimulant, the same loadstone, the same fell fascination that the woman of fashion found in the London of pleasure!

Cruel curse of centralisation, drawing the strength of the nation into slums and alleys to press it to death like rotten, overcrowded, ill-packed fruits! Better the death of a sheep frozen on a snow-covered moor, better even the fate of a shot hare falling on the ferns amongst the bluebell and the foxglove in the grass; better anything, any shape of suffering or of want, of trouble or of travail, in the dew-wet rural fields, and the green combes and valleys, within sound of the mill sluices and within reach of the strong west winds, than that sickening suicide of soul and body, the life of the poor in the city of London!

Flodden heard a great deal talked about the poor. He saw Violet Guernsey going off to the East-end with her Spanish guitar and her baritones and tenors from the Household Brigade; he heard Lady Maltby speak unctuously of her tea parties for her dear brothers and sisters from Limehouse and Shoreditch;

he was invited by the Duchess of Worthing
to go to her Penny Readings in Mile End, and
was offered his choice between a Bab Ballad
and an Ingoldsby Legend to be the means
whereby he should touch the hearts and
awaken the smiles of ' those nice queer people,'
the stevedores and dock labourers and bargees
and mudlarks.

He had seen fashion and riches playing at
patronage and popularity with the poor as
blindly as, but more clumsily than, poor
Marie Antoinette had once played at them;
and he had seen men of tricky talent riding
the hobby-horse of philanthropy to canter
upon it up park avenues and through castle
doors which they would never have entered
had they not bestridden that useful steed.
He had seen the poor trotted out and dressed
up and held forth as pretence and excuse for
everything; used by the great lady's ennui,
by the politician's party motives, by the news-
paper-writer's spleen, by the novelist's need
of sensation, by the adventurer's greed and
ambition, by the Conservative's desire to appear a benefactor, and the Radical's anxiety
to seem a patriot; made by all a toy, a tool,
a bone of contention, a stalking horse, a pretext, a weapon, or a boast, from the Primrose

dame who wanted a ballot on earth and a place in heaven, to the Editor who found charity cover a multitude of sins and sell ten thousand copies of a slanderous journal.

But it seemed to him, as he walked sadly homeward in the early evening, that all those who thus traded in and toyed with this gigantic woe, this endless horror, knew not what they did, and mocked at and insulted it when they came, with their cheap nostrums and charlatans' panaceas, to cure this hopeless cancer in the body politic.

CHAPTER XXXIX

THAT afternoon Beaufront heard a rumour which displeased him highly: he said nothing as he heard it, but walked out of the club in which he was at the time, and went with long swift strides up the staircase of the St. James's Hotel.

'Is it true that you are leaving town?' he asked without preface, as he entered Syrlin's apartments.

'I am leaving England,' replied Syrlin equally curtly.

The reply had an aggressive sound in it which grated on his friend's ear.

'I think, under the circumstances, it would be better if you stayed here a little time longer,' said Beaufront very slowly, in the tone of a man who desires his words to be marked but not offensive.

'Under what circumstances?'

Beaufront hesitated; his rule, the common rule of society, never to intrude advice, or interfere with any private sentiments, made him doubtful as to his reply. But the candour natural to him, and the irritation which he felt, conquered his habits of neutrality.

'Under the circumstances of your romantic rescue of Lady Avillion,' he answered deliberately. 'The thing was well done, I do not deny it, but it was perhaps more sensational than it need have been, and my cousin is a very well known person, one of those persons everybody talks about. Under the circumstances, I repeat, it seems to me better that you should stay on and fulfil your social engagements here, as her own health has necessitated her leaving England.'

Syrlin looked at him with a sombre insolence brooding in his dark eyes.

'What is your title to say so?'

'Oh, my dear Syrlin, I make no pretensions to any title; but you are an old and dear friend of mine, my cousin is a near and dear relative, and I make no apology whatever for telling you distinctly that I object to an imprudence on your part which will accentuate a series of imprudences which you have committed of late, wholly unintentional no doubt, but still unwisely.'

'You are *plus royaliste que le roi!* I

have just seen Lord Avillion at the Marlborough, and he said to me " How wise you are to get away! " I cannot for a moment admit that my humble personality can possibly be connected with the actions of so great a lady as your cousin.'

' I never said that it was,' said Beaufront ; ' but though you did a gallant thing you did it—well,—sensationally, and it was the talk of the town a very little while ago, and I do not consider that you have any right to recall attention to it by leaving London suddenly just because she has left it.'

' Why does not her husband say so ? '

' Her husband could not say so if he thought it.'

Syrlin coloured with anger and with the unwelcome sense that what was said was true.

' You do me too much honour in imagining that I have any power to compromise her ! '

' You have the power to attract injurious constructions upon her, because you were associated with her in a public scene, in a public danger, and because you have for months, whether you know it or not, made your admiration of her the *secret de Polichinelle* to all London.'

Syrlin's face grew red with a hot colour like a woman's.

In the customary blindness of passion he had imagined his feelings to be wholly concealed from others; with the temperament of a poet he had the indiscretion of one, and because his lips were silent never dreamed that his eyes betrayed him. He was humiliated and embarrassed by the reproof which he received; he felt like some immature student rebuked by a man of the world. He was strongly attached to Beaufront, and he knew what Beaufront said was true; at the same time the quickness of his passion and the hauteur of his temper made him least able of all men to brook such interference from anyone.

'If we were in France—' he muttered.

Beaufront laughed a little.

'My dear boy! you would send me your *témoins*? You would do a useless thing. We should probably kill each other, because we are both of equal force in those amusements, and the world would certainly not talk less, but more. You are not the man I have supposed you if you take roughly what I say. My cousin, Lady Avillion, is a beautiful woman with the glare of the world shed upon her; she is a very noble and innocent person, and I do not think that a friend of mine, a dear friend, and one whom I myself presented to her, should be the means of gathering about her that kind of impertinent scandal from which so few conspicuous people escape nowadays, but which has never approached her hitherto, thanks to her own admirable judgment and consummate discretion. That is all I have to say. I am responsible to myself for having made you acquainted with her.'

Syrlin felt the deepest displeasure and the keenest mortification as he listened; the justice of Beaufront's censure was beyond all question, and struck him with a mortifying sense that he who had a few moments before rebuked that raw Scotch lad for his incautious follies, seemed himself as indiscreet and as unwise in another man's sight, and possibly in that of the whole of society.

All the Spanish and semi-Oriental blood of Syrlin was at boiling point; he was a spoilt child of the world; he was habituated to take his own way and never lacked adorers who told him that it was the right way; he had the haughty temper of princes in his veins joined to a morbid susceptibility which had always made him over-ready to resent any slight or slur, even to imagine such when they were not intended. But he had also strong affections, and that willingness to acknowledge error which belongs to mobile and generous temperaments. He was attached to Beaufront; he had had cause to be grateful to him in earlier years; all his knowledge of the world told him that what Beaufront said now was, however unwelcome, wholly true.

Like many men suddenly possessed and swayed by a strong passion, he had had no idea that his feelings and sentiments were so visible to others. The recent cordiality of her lord had seemed to him a guarantee that not the faintest suspicion could have entered into the mind of anyone as to the real nature of his feelings for Lady Avillion.

Although impassioned and headstrong, those feelings were so exalted, and so imbued with the noblest kind of devotion, that it hurt him intolerably to realise that they were the subject of observation and remark to anyone. He had been utterly unconscious of the many evidences of his devotion which he had so recklessly given to the world, and the consciousness of his own thoughtlessness was very bitter to him.

'And I repeat,' he said now sullenly, 'that Lord Avillion is the only person who has the right to object to my acquaintance with her.'

'Lord Avillion will not object,' replied Beaufront. 'There is such a phrase in English as an event suiting one's book. *I* object; and as I like plain speaking I tell you so in plain words.'

'And I deny your authority to use such words or express such objections.'

'Your denial will not affect the facts,' said Beaufront coldly. 'It appears to me that we are approaching something very like a quarrel. I do not want or wish to quarrel with you, but I tell you that you shall not compromise my cousin while I am alive. I took you to her house, and you are responsible to me for any abuse of the privilege of her acquaintance, if you do abuse it.'

'You are in love with Lady Avillion yourself!' said Syrlin bitterly.

Beaufront smiled rather mournfully.

'I have long ceased to be; but if I were so I should not carry my heart on my sleeve as you do. There are pecking daws all over the place, why please and feed them?'

Syrlin turned from him, and walked up and down the room with a fury in his heart which he strove to control. What Beaufront asked from him was a sacrifice wholly alien to his natural habits. He was used to follow every impulse as a child follows a butterfly flying down a sunny road. It was intolerable to him to remain where the idol of his thoughts was not. He had no definite purpose, he did not dare to define his wishes, even to himself, lest, like snow crystals, they should crumble at a touch. He had the deep humility of every great passion. He never presumed to think that he should become greatly necessary to her, but to be near her, to watch her movements, to hear the sound of her voice, to divine her wishes, her sentiments, her sorrows, from her mere chance words, all this had become absolutely necessary to him; he felt that there was a part of her nature which was visible to, which belonged to, himself alone. It was not in his creeds or in his habits to feel thus for a woman and deny himself the sweetness of vicinity to her. He had more honour and less self-indulgence than most men who, in the flower of their age, have the world at their feet, but he was no ascetic and no moralist.

What Beaufront asked of him was a simple and plain act of self-denial; and it was one alien to him, and odious, doubly odious because dictated to him by another.

He was jealous of the very air that she breathed, of the trees in whose shade she walked, of the music which fell on her ear, of the dog she caressed, of the flower she wore; it was such love as he had sung of in his song 'La Reine pleurait;' romantic, unreasoning, uncalculating, at once spiritual and impassioned, at once a religion and a desire. His position was one in which to persist was disloyal, and to desist was humiliating: he had no possible right to compromise Lady Avillion, and he knew that had he been in Beaufront's place he would have spoken as Beaufront spoke, and he hated himself for having inadvertently disclosed the closest and deepest sentiment of his life. His habits were self-indulgent and his passions were wilful and capricious; he had in him the intolerance of control and the headstrong impulses of race and of genius, and to endure dictation on such a delicate and sensitive feeling as his secret adoration of a woman was intolerable to him. But he was sincere, and he was very susceptible to any appeal to his honour.

After a few minutes' silence he turned to Beaufront without anger.

'I admit that you are justified in saying what you do. I should probably say the same in your place. If you consider that my departure at this moment could be construed injuriously to Lady Avillion, though I have not the presumption to think so, I will remain in England some weeks longer. I should never have supposed that society would do me the honour to connect my departure with hers, but if you consider there is any fear of this, I will demur to your apprehensions.'

There was a tone of condescension and a certain amount of insolence in the apparent docility of the reply which grated on Beaufront as he heard it; but he had gained his point, and he did not think it politic to quarrel with how he gained it.

'Thanks,' he said briefly, and he held out his hand to Syrlin.

'*Ah, pour cela non!*' said Syrlin with a strong vibration of indignant emotion in his voice, as he held his hands behind his back. 'I defer to your demands because they are just; but you are no longer my friend, although I will never be your enemy.'

And with that he left the room before Beaufront could reply or detain him.

'Oh those artists, what froward children they are!' thought Beaufront with mingled amusement and annoyance as, left alone in the apartment, he glanced at the masses of flowers, the litter of costly and artistic objects, the piles of letters, some unopened, some torn in two, the Erard grand pianoforte, the antique weapons, the cabinet pictures, the writing table with panels by Fragonard and bronzes by Gouthière which Syrlin had bought at Christie's to give a look of grace and comfort to the gorgeous but naked hotel drawing-room, with its roar and rattle of Piccadilly, rising up from the stones below.

'What children they are!' he thought again, as he took his hat and left the apartments. He had been ostensibly the victor in this interview, but he had an uneasy sense that success would not ultimately be with him. He believed that Syrlin's estrangement from him would not be of long duration; he considered it rather a petulant insolence than a serious menace, and bestowed no thought upon it. But though he did not regret what he had said, he vaguely felt that the efficacy of any words or acts of his in this matter would be doubtful.

'*On ne peut pas être plus royaliste que le roi.*'

It could not long be possible for him effectually to resent for Avillion what Avillion did not resent for himself.

CHAPTER XL

A WEEK or two later he learned to his great astonishment and annoyance that Syrlin had purchased the estate called Willowsleigh at Richmond; a beautifully wooded though small place, with a house built in the eighteenth century and many stories attached to it of pageantries, masquerades, wits, dandies, and royalties.

'I had better have let him leave England when he wanted to do so,' thought Beaufront; conscious, as most of us are when we meddle with others, that abstinence from advice or remark is the only sure, if the most selfish, form of wisdom. That Syrlin, a man who was ill at ease when he was not wandering over Europe, Asia, or Africa, a man with the temperament of an artist, the unrest of a Bohemian, and the mingled ennui and esprit of a child of Paris, should take even temporary root in England, seemed to him incredible.

Willowsleigh was a picturesque, historic, and interesting place, but it was commonplace beside the Tourelle of Louis d'Orléans at St. Germains, prosaic and modern and dull and damp when compared to those Moorish towns and villages amidst the palms and aloes of African shores in which Syrlin loved to renew the dreams of his boyhood. It was now, indeed, in all its midsummer profusion of foliage, and the Thames flowed by it broad and calm in morning and evening mists. But it was a place of which Syrlin would tire in a day unless some strong magnetism or motive bound him to it. The newspapers were full of details of the purchase, of the fêtes which would be given at it, of the compliment paid to the country by the choice of so famous and capricious an artist; and Beaufront as he glanced angrily over all these paragraphs had a mortified sense of having been foiled with his own rapier and hoist with his own petard. Meanwhile Syrlin spent the long cloudy summer days, with their sad and seemingly unending twilight hours, in the damp green gardens and the grey willow copses of his own home. The house was situated on a backwater of the Thames, and was removed from all the river-traffic and clamour of the river-highway. Great

beds of rushes and osiers grew beneath its banks,
and trout and dace glittered and swans floated
under the heavy shadows of its planes and
cedars. It lay low, it was cloudy and dusky
and humid, and seemed more so even than it
was to eyes that were used to the clear sunshine of Central Europe and the strong hot
light of Africa. But its deep green glades,
its rich water-meadows, its silent shadowy
paths winding under canopies of dense foliage
with a gleam of shining water at their close,
suited, for the moment at least, the deep sad-
ness of his thoughts, and soothed the intense
impatience of his spirit. She was absent, and
he was told that he could not follow her
without causing increase to that injurious
chatter and comment already set in motion
by his own imprudences. It was melancholy,
at least its grey dull water, its deep shade
of cedar and willow, its frequent river-mists,
seemed so to this son of warmer lands; but
there was something in its shadows and
silence which was sympathetic to his moods,
although opposed to them. It was in scenery
what Gray's Elegy is in verse—soft, classic,
elegant, subdued. It was not like anything
that he had ever known: it was cool and
passionless and restricted and melancholy,

as all English scenery always is; but it was tender and serene; its absolute contrast to his own mood attracted whilst it reproached him. He had that intolerance of the movement of the world, that detestation of all ordinary companionship, that impatience and indifference to all public life and social demands which come with the absorption of all strong passions. Since for the moment he must not be near her, he chose to be with no one, to have nothing break in upon the consecration of his memories and meditations to her.

He wondered sometimes what Avillion thought.

But the thoughts of Avillion were seldom to be read by anyone. One evening, in the Marlborough, there had been some talk of the purchase when Avillion was present, but he had said little except to wonder if Syrlin would have his pastels sent over. He had a very fine collection of eighteenth-century pastels in the Avenue Josephine, even some of La Tour's amongst them. Avillion knew the collection very well, and opined that it would be more in its epoch at the Richmond house than in the Paris one; the De Goncourts were so right in urging the consideration of epochs; most collectors nowadays made such an appaling jumble of their things. The St. Germains tower was correct, quite extraordinarily correct, he said, considering the immense difficulty of finding art and furniture of that date; he supposed Syrlin would show the same correctness of choice in arranging this eighteenth-century English house. And those were all the observations he made on the matter.

Beaufront, on the contrary, was deeply and justifiably angered. He felt that his friend and favourite had dealt unkindly with him, had defeated, and in a way outwitted him. He was well aware that Syrlin by remaining in England intended to show to him that he was wholly indifferent to his opinion and wholly careless of his counsels, and had yielded on one point, only to do what was more undesired, more invidious; and yet what it was impossible to challenge or prevent.

It was impossible to quarrel with anyone for having bought property which it was a national gain should be purchased by a person of cultured taste who would preserve its natural beauties from the curse of the jerry-builder and the market-gardener. It was equally impossible to allow it to appear that he foresaw in any man's residence in the country any possible danger to the peace or the reputation of a member of his own family, or admit that the presence of any stranger in the country could compromise her, or constitute any danger or source of injury to her.

There was an obstinacy and an ingenuity in the action of Syrlin which profoundly irritated and displeased him, and he felt his own impotence to resent it or to alter it.

'The river fogs will ruin his voice, that is one consolation,' he thought in his wrath. 'The low shores of the Thames for a man born at Ceuta and chilly as a nervous woman!'

But in his affections Syrlin had long held a place too firmly for any acts or words of his to dislodge him from it; and Beaufront had affections as tenacious and as warm as they were usually reticent in expression.

'Something ruffles you—what is it?' said Consuelo Laurence to him. She knew him so well that any variation in his moods was visible to her.

'I am annoyed that you will never come to any of my houses,' he said, with one of those half-truths in which the most sensible men will at times take refuge.

'That is so old a story I cannot believe in its distressing you at this moment,' she answered him. 'I do not even believe that you wish it when none of your women will know me.'

'Know you! They all speak to you.'

'Oh, my dear Ralph! There is a way of speaking to one which is rather more slighting than not to speak at all. That is Lady Avillion's and her sister's and your sister's way of speaking to me. I do not complain of it; I should probably do the same or worse in their place. I can always understand people's dislike. When they like me it seems far more wonderful.'

'And when they love you, you do not believe in it!' said Beaufront in a low and almost sullen voice.

'I believe that they deceive themselves,' she answered very tranquilly. 'What vexes you now is this story of Syrlin and Lady Avillion. But I think you are very unjust. She would probably have been very much injured if no one had cared to leave the comfortable security of the Bachelors' windows to go down and join the fray.'

'I was not at the Bachelors',' said Beaufront angrily. 'I was down at Delamere that week.'

'I know you were. I have always envied Lady Avillion, but I never envied her so much as I did that day. It must be such a delightful reflection to have had a great occasion and been equal to it. Your world is full of pin-pricks and mosquito bites, but it very seldom allows anyone the luxury of a great occasion.'

'He has made the most of his occasion,' said Beaufront moodily. 'He makes everything sensational that he touches.'

'How can you say so! He is ever utterly unwilling to speak of the scene.'

'That is only an affected attitude,' said Beaufront, with an ill-nature of which even on the utterance he felt ashamed.

Consuelo Laurence smiled.

'You are all of you ill-natured to your idol since the Hyde Park riot. I daresay anyone of you would have done as much as he did, only it occurred to nobody but himself.'

'What vile motives you attribute to one! I am angry, if you wish really to know why, because he wants to go out of town just because my cousin is gone, and I have quarrelled with him about it.'

'Surely you should have left that to her husband?'

'Her husband would not quarrel with him

if he carried her off to Morocco. Uther is in love with Mme. du Charolois.'

' What a droll complication ! ' said Consuelo Laurence with slight sympathy.

Beaufront said nothing ; he was moodily silent and grave, playing with the ears of his colley dog, and glancing at Consuelo Laurence from under his drooped eyelids. How cool and fair and serene she looked ! How well she would become the galleries and glades of Heronsmere ! Why would she erect all these impassable barriers, all these fantastic obstacles between himself and her?

' My dear Consuelo, let us leave other people alone and speak of ourselves,' he said abruptly. ' You know very well that in those old days I never doubted you, never failed to give you my full esteem and respect ; why should you suppose that I should do less if you belonged to me ? '

' It could not be the same thing,' she said sadly. ' You have been most good to me always, but then I have *not* belonged to you, and for that very reason you could do me justice dispassionately. After all, you have believed in me rather from the chivalry of your temper than from anything that you have really known for certain.'

'I have believed in you because I am not a fool.'

'Well, put it so; but in our friendship there has been nothing which would have made it really matter much to you had your belief been wrong. Therefore no suspicions have disturbed it. If I were your wife it would matter so intensely to you, that inevitable suspicions would incessantly occur to you; and the wife of a man of great position must be like Cæsar's.'

'Cæsar demanded a good deal more than he gave; he was a beast in his own morals.'

'Was he? He was right about his wife for all that. You have believed in all I told you of myself, but I have given you no proof of it; no woman can give proofs of that sort, especially when she has had a *vie orageuse* like mine.'

Beaufront listened with ill-concealed and intense impatience.

'You talk as if you were Messalina. Why will you do it? You pain me, you irritate me, and you calumniate yourself.'

'No, dear; I am not Messalina. But if I took you at your word, a year hence, a month hence, you would begin pondering restlessly on all I have told you, and wondering, despite yourself, whether or not it were true.'

'What a poor, white-livered, self-tormenting idiot you would make me out to be!'

'Not at all. But you are an Englishman, and every Englishman is at heart conventional. You are a man of high rank, in the full blaze of the world's observation; it would be intolerable for you to think that the Duchess of Beaufront had ever sung at a café chantant.'

'Should I ever have known of that if you had not voluntarily told me?'

'Probably not, but that would make no difference. What is most painful and pathetic in human relations is that the voluntary confession of a woman constantly sows the seeds of suspicion of her in the minds of men who care for her. Candour is the virtue for which we pay most dearly.'

'No one repents it with me.'

'I know that you are unusually generous and wholly to be trusted. But I know too that you are much prouder than you are in the least degree aware of, and that it would be intolerable to you for society to depreciate your wife.'

'But society is at your feet!'

'At my feet in a sense; it has accepted me as a woman of fashion. But do you suppose that I am not discussed and condemned in half a hundred houses the moment I have left their drawing-rooms? All that does not affect you in the least as my friend; but as—my husband—it would be wholly unendurable to you.'

A slight wave of colour passed over her delicate cheeks as she spoke; Beaufront looked at her with that sense of powerlessness which unnerves the strongest before arguments which are drawn from conclusions as to the future. Such arguments are at once intangible and indestructible; phantom hosts whose force is greater because impalpable. Who can be sure that he will not do or feel such and such a thing in the future?

He rose and leaned against the mantelpiece beside her, looking down upon her with a prolonged gaze which embarrassed her.

'Consuelo—trust me,' he said very earnestly. 'I cannot argue with you, no man can argue coldly with a woman he loves, but trust me; you shall never repent it.'

'You do not love me,' she said quickly. 'You love Lady Avillion.'

'That is your fixed idea. It is absurd.'

His countenance grew harsh and his voice was stern; his eyes looked away from her across the room towards the green gloom of the palms and ferns.

A little sigh escaped Consuelo Laurence.

'I know you better than you know yourself,' she said gently. 'If she were free tomorrow you would offer to marry her. Keep yourself free, at least, my dear. And now please ring for tea; I have been driving all day and I am thirsty.'

He obeyed her; he walked to where the electric button of the bell was and touched it; then he stood in moody silence in front of her; she looked up at him a little timidly.

'Let us always be friends just the same,' she said wistfully.

Beaufront laughed.

'That is so like a woman; she throws a vase down and breaks it and says, " Let us believe it is whole again, that will do just as well."'

She was pained by his tone.

'There is nothing broken with us, or there need be nothing broken. What is there changed? Nothing. You have said things to me which it will be my wish and my duty to forget; but a moment's—difference of opinion—cannot obliterate seven years of friendship and esteem.'

Beaufront said nothing; he was wondering if she spoke sincerely; all these years he had never doubted her sincerity, he had even proved it many times; but now her calmness and her indifference seemed to him like duplicity.

'A moment's difference of opinion!' he thought with great anger. 'That is how a woman sets aside a man's wish to pass his life beside her! And then they say we are too *légers*! Good heavens!'

'You are offended with me,' said Consuelo, regretfully. 'I am sorry, so sorry. But it is easier to bear with your irritation now than it would be to watch you gradually becoming more and more embittered at the knowledge that you had irrevocably sacrificed your future.'

'What sentimental trash!' he cried with suppressed fury. 'Who attaches all that importance to marriage nowadays? Not a soul!'

'I do. *J'ai passé par là*, and I know that, however slight a matter it seems, it is like a thorn in the foot, like a pin in the flesh, it destroys all the joy of living. I will not spoil your life; you have deserved better of me than that. This is a moment of impulse and fancy with you; it will pass, and we shall be as good friends as we have always been since that March evening—do you remember it?—when you came into my little salon in the Rue Rouget de Lisle, and found me by my poor little dying Margot. Pray—pray—my dear Ralph—do not let *us* quarrel. Friendship is surer than love; sympathy is better than marriage.'

There was emotion in her voice as though for a very little more her tears would have choked it; but Beaufront for once was not touched, he looked at her with harshness and impatience and scepticism.

'Women can live on their d—d empty sentiment, as they live on ice cream and a cup of tea,' he said savagely. 'They will keep a man on their own regimen and forget that he hungers and thirsts and starves.'

'My dear Ralph!'— She looked at him with embarrassment and some offence, and added with a touch of derision, 'That you can starve through me is wholly impossible. This fancy of yours is wholly new and baseless. If you dislike my sentimentality of feeling, I must confess that I do not like your coarseness of language. But you may say what you please and I shall never resent it, because I owe you vast debts for a kindness which has never failed me until now. I shall not quarrel with you, however you may provoke me to quarrel. I stand between you and an *entêtement* of the moment. The time will come when you will do my motives justice. Until then, do not let us make food for the idle chatter of gossipers by any alteration in our manner to one another, or our daily habits of acquaintanceship. When people gain nothing by making the world talk, it is absurd to do so.'

'Your prudence and your philosophy are admirable and enviable, and leave my uncouthness far behind them,' said Beaufront savagely. 'I had better go to the Cape or the Pole with my schooner. Then no one can possibly say anything.'

He looked at her, hoping that she would offer some remonstrance or objection; but she made none. She continued to embroider a gold bird on the black satin.

'You would care nothing, I believe, if I went down in a monsoon off the Horn!' he muttered with a fierce reproach.

A look of pain passed over her face, but

she stooped over the gold threads of her embroidery, and he did not see it; he thought that she bent her head to hide a smile. And with no other word, and without any sign of adieu, he went out of the room, flinging aside the satin of the door hangings with a savage gesture.

Consuelo's eyes filled with tears; she let the bullion threads fall on her lap and pushed the screen away. All the sweet quiet, pleasant intercourse of the past was over between them; all the repose of their candid and confidential friendship was ruined and scattered as a child's sand castle by an incoming tide. She knew much of the passions of men, and had often been their object, and she dreaded and disliked them; she knew the frowardness of passion, its unkindness, its caprice, its unreason, its rapid descent from the height of adoration into the slough of satiety. Why must this restless, unreasoning, wayward folly come to disturb that serene and constant sympathy which it had been so long her pride to preserve untroubled by any other feeling?

'And he only wishes it because it is denied him!' she thought sadly, with that knowledge of men's temperaments and impulses which leaves the woman who has it no possibility of illusion as to the feelings she inspires.

Beaufront went down Wilton Street that day in pain and anger.

Consuelo Laurence looked after him, unseen herself, where she stood in the shelter of the red and white awning and broad-leaved palms of her balcony, where lobelias, and canariensis, and noisette roses, were running over in foam of blossom.

'Ah, my dear!' she thought, 'for you, of all men on earth, to imagine that you would never trouble yourself what the world would say of your wife! No man in the whole world would be more intolerant of the very slightest shadow falling on his escutcheon, or the very smallest doubt being raised about anyone who belonged to him!'

She gazed after him with a sigh as he walked down the street, in what chanced to be full sunshine that afternoon.

'What use,' she thought, 'is it to love anyone, unless one loves them for themselves and not for ourselves?'

Wilton Street is a short street, and he was soon out of sight; but she remained on the balcony amongst the flowers, thinking sadly and painfully, whilst in the green trees by the church opposite the sparrows twittered and fluttered in their usual happy insouciance. She was a generous woman, and persisted in her own self-sacrifice, but such sacrifice is hard, and made the future seem to her long, and tedious, and joyless.

'What a lovely woman she is!' said an American girl who did not know her, looking at her that night in the stalls at the French play. 'And what a lucky one!'

'You bet!' said an American matron. 'Why, my child, I remember that woman selling oysters on the quay at Charlestown, and now you're hearing 'em all say she'll die a duchess. If we sent tinned peas over here and called 'em pearls, these dudes 'd buy 'em, and wear 'em too!'

The Duchess of Kincardine and Oronsay chanced to be in the stall next to this lady, and carried on the remark, which she overheard, to a great house where there was a ball.

'Mrs. Laurence sold oysters in the streets before she went in for the café chantant business,' said that excellent dowager a dozen times in the evening. 'Yes; I had it on the best authority, Americans who know it for a fact!'

CHAPTER XLI

'*Il boude!*' thought Avillion with a slow smile on hearing of Willowsleigh, the retirement of his enemy from the world. It was not exactly what he wanted; it was a lull in the drama, like an entr'acte; but, as in an entr'acte, he talked with pretty women, visited the green-room, smoked some cigarettes, glanced at the evening news in the corridors, so he was by no means so engrossed in the spectacle of Syrlin's actions as to be indifferent to the many distractions and solicitations which throng about the person of a man of rank and riches who has also a handsome face and an open hand. Crowds of people were always ready to amuse him, or to speak more exactly, to amuse in him that mild critical mood of passing good-humour which, half bored, half beguiled, was the utmost approach he ever made to genuine pleasure in anything.

He hated Syrlin with a sound hatred

based on offended dignity and misplaced calculations; but even hatred could take a passive form in him, and he could understand those murderers who poisoned people very slowly. He never forgave an affront. Being of the high position he was, he indeed seldom received one; but when he did he would no more have forgiven it than a pope could forgive a person who kissed his hand.

It was only indiscreet women who amused, pleased, or occupied him in society; but that the faintest shade of indiscretion should be visible in a woman who was before the world as his wife struck him as the most infamous wrong to himself.

'I never cared for her after three months,' he thought with indignation. 'But I always admired her, and I thought her most perfectly safe!'

So, in the entr'acte he remained for July in London, July being the month when the weather was least odious; and remained the more willingly because at the last State concert of the year he had seen a lady for whom he had conceived an immediate and violent admiration.

Despite the many offences to public opinion of which he was guilty, he was always desirous of conciliating public opinion. He would have detested to be classed as a *mauvais sujet*; a certain deference to social rules was in his view indispensable to good breeding. The Upper House, the Court, the Privy Council, even St. James's Chapel, saw him in his place at them whenever his appearance was really necessary either in duty or in etiquette. In ordinary mortals he would have called this snobbism, but in himself he regarded it as virtue and as propriety. A morbid desire to stand well in the eyes of others may exist in the same breast that harbours the most arrogant pride and scorn. Avillion, though he considered no one his equal except princes of the blood, would yet have been uneasy and mortified if the poorest curate near Brakespeare had preached a sermon against him. It is a very common English characteristic, and has its uses to the community at large, though it is neither honest nor admirable. It was because his wife had so thoroughly understood the necessity of conciliating opinion that she had so conduced to the serenity of his existence. Avillion always observed the letter of the social law; it allowed him to break it in the spirit more completely and comfortably. It is indeed marvellous what unlimited con-

cessions may be obtained from others by those
who pursue such a policy. He considered,
and wisely, that social consideration is a
necessary appanage to rank. So he bored
himself to grace various formalities and
ceremonies attendant on the close of the
season; and at one of these he had been
rewarded by the sight of a new beauty, the
Duchesse de Charolois.

She was a very lovely person, daughter of
the Prince de Créci, and widow, before she
was twenty, of one of the greatest nobles of
France.

She was the idol of the immediate hour
in London; her manner, her history, and
her peculiar style of beauty being all enhanced by the long seclusion in which
she had been wholly withdrawn from the
world since the death by a fall in hunting
of the young Duke to whom she had been
wedded almost in childhood. She made
those who had any small learning think of
the devout and lovely women who had
buried themselves at Port Royal. She
was extremely handsome, with classic features, large mournful eyes under dreamy
lids, and a complexion of surpassing trans-
parency and delicacy. To this she united a

beautiful figure, great height, and a perfect manner, very still, languid, and full of grace. These beauties, with the knowledge that she was wholly indifferent to the world and insensible to homage, aroused in the breast of Avillion an admiration which was the stronger because of a kind quite unusual with him. She was a person whom it was impossible to approach without the profoundest respect, and as with all women whom he was compelled to respect, he had usually by choice had only a bowing acquaintance, the fascination of this novel sentiment was extreme. It was the one thing needed to complete the growing anger and dislike with which he viewed his wife.

If he were only free!

It had never happened to him before to be checked by his position in any amorous fancy, although his imaginary captivity was an interesting theme for his lamentations in conversation with women who pleased him. But now, his marriage actually did stand in his way, and prevent any possibility of his sentiments being even hinted to the young Duchess, who was well known to be reserved to hauteur and religious asceticism.

'My whole life has been overshadowed

by irremediable circumstances,' he murmured once, in a tone which suggested the innumerable confidences which only a sense of delicacy and of duty caused him to withhold.

'You do not look a victim to adverse circumstances,' said the Duchess with a smile.

'You are pleased to make light of what I suffer,' he said with resignation, but a suggestion of injury permitted to mingle with it. 'I do not pretend to more than I feel. *On se console de tout, plus ou moins bien.* But you mistake if you, like the world, believe me a mere heartless pleasure-seeker to whom the sympathies and solace of an intimate affection would not have been very dear—could I have enjoyed them.'

'What should prevent your enjoying them?' replied the lady unmoved. 'Lady Avillion is surely all that the most fastidious could desire.'

'My wife is perfect,' said Avillion in a soft slow tone, which implied the exact contrary to his words. 'Quite perfect. But she is cold. Anyone may see that.'

'It is fortunate for you that she is so, for if rumour speaks correctly she might have given you many a troublesome moment had she been more exacting!'

'When ever *does* rumour speak correctly?' said Avillion with a sigh. 'What does society know of us? It only sees us with our armour on and our visors down. My wife is an admirable person; she is quite faultless indeed, but sometimes imperfection is more amiable than perfection, or at all events more indulgent. No one,' he added with a sigh, 'is indulgent who does not care for the offender.'

'Perhaps you have offended too often and so have worn out her indulgence,' said the Duchess, yielding a little despite herself to the charm of the sweet and melancholy regard and accent.

'Oh no! she never cared,' replied Avillion, who had so entirely entered into the part he assumed of a man *mal compris* that he had almost by this time persuaded himself that it was his real character.

The Duchess raised her languid lids and looked at him with surprise and a vague interest; but she knew the world and knew all that it attributed to him.

'You are very unfortunate,' she said in a tone which she intended to be unkind. 'But I scarcely think it is fair to Lady Avillion to discuss her want of heart or of comprehension with a stranger. It is not *she* whom the world accuses of *légèretés.*'

Then she gave him a little bend of her head and turned away, leaving him, by the sheer contradiction of human nature, more really enamoured of her than he had been for many years of anyone.

But he had so far succeeded with her that, although displeasure and disapproval were foremost in her mind, there was beside these a certain wonder as to whether by any chance he could have been speaking the truth to her, and could really be unhappy in his private relations. No woman, however well she knows mankind and their hypocrisies, is altogether proof against the charm which lies in the confidence of a seductive and accomplished person who insinuates that everyone else except herself misjudges him, and that all judgment except her own is indifferent to him. The subtlest compliment to a woman is to make her feel that she alone is the confessional to which a man can reveal his veritable and actual self.

Mme. de Charolois fully believed that Avillion was merely playing a part, yet she was not quite sure that it was all untrue; there was just that slight curiosity about him, that vague inclination to take interest in what he had told her, which is the surest of all sentiments to increase and to expand.

She thought it an offence to good taste for him to blame his wife to her; she did not in the least credit that he was to be pitied or that his wife was to be blamed, and yet he had so great a charm about him and such extreme perfection of untruth, that her interest in what he had hinted was stronger than her condemnation of his semi-revelations.

Avillion could always gain over anyone to his side when he desired, and although few men living had treated women more brutally than he, none had more defenders than he amongst women, even amongst those whom he had treated the worst. Moreover, in his present censure of his wife he had a great advantage; it was something wholly new; he had habitually praised and honoured his wife to the ear of everyone and rendered her by his words what he took from her by his actions; and therefore the part he played now to the Duchess de Charolois had great freshness and fascination in it for him as well as for his audience. It amused him whilst it almost beguiled him into belief in it himself. He began to persuade himself that if only ten years ago Freda had been more sympathetic, more pliable, he would have been quite blameless in his relations to her; she was a great coquette, cold though she was; she had never endeavoured to understand him; she had been always absorbed in society and politics; she had really been the first to withdraw herself. It was a novel and entertaining situation for him; he persuaded himself that he was a man of feeling, altogether misunderstood and sacrificed. His irritation against his wife increased in proportion as his admiration for Mme. de Charolois acquired strength and sincerity, and he found a zest in this confusion of sentiments greater than any that his facile conquests had of late afforded him.

English country-houses are the scenes and shelter of many illicit enjoyments. and he exercised his tact and ingenuity in arranging his visits to them so as to coincide with hers. He was so rarely in England at this season, and so very rarely was to be persuaded into visiting his peers, that his acceptance of these invitations was a great glory, anxiety, and pleasure to those he honoured. It was well known that he liked no houses except his own, and was bored to death almost everywhere; therefore naturally he was inordinately coveted as a guest by those who were hopeless of ever possibly pleasing him.

A person whose sole and exclusive aim is to be amused will, if he possess the power to gratify all his caprices, seldom fail to render it impossible for anyone to amuse him; and the perfect politeness which veiled Avillion's dissatisfaction only rendered it more painfully apparent to those on whom the duty devolved of dissipating it.

Avillion was never rude, never ungracious; he was urbanity itself to anyone who did not belong to him; but he had an expression of resigned yet unspeakable ennui which struck terror into the souls of his entertainers, and fell like ice on the circle around him; whilst to ' hint a fault and hesitate dislike ' was an art in which he had reached the finest perfection.

Under the reforming influences of his new passion, he was this year inspired by a fit of patriotism, of insularity as he was wont to call patriotism when displayed by other Englishmen. He went to Buxton instead of to Carlsbad, and intended to go to Doncaster instead of to Baden. Being gifted with that kind of mind (such a pleasure to those who possess it) which easily enabled him to see and think what he wished to see and think, he persuaded himself that he had always liked English life.

'Pray don't believe what they tell you of me,' he murmured plaintively to the Duchess. 'I am a slave to duty, a slave!'

And he really believed it himself.

'No man works harder than I do when I am in my county,' he assured her, 'or when I am in town. I ought now, if I considered my health, to be at Bogesloev in Moravia; you know they have discovered the most miraculous spring there; ferruginous, and much stronger in iodine than any known spring in the world; it would do me an immensity of good. But at this juncture one is bound to stay here and do what one can for the country; things never were worse; and we are drifting straight to Communism, to the most frightfully vulgar Communism; yet still one must struggle on against it to the last.'

His way of struggling on against it was to subscribe a thousand a year to a pack of hounds of which he never saw even the tips of their tails; to distribute another thousand between the parochial schools and those of the town nearest Brakespeare, seeing as little of the scholars as he did of the hounds; to subscribe more magnificently still to the Carlton, and attend there occasionally if the Premier convened an especial meeting of the Party; and once at least every season to entertain splendidly at his castle the Bishop and the Dean, the Lord Lieutenant and the Deputy, the High Sheriff, and the country gentlemen. There are, perhaps, less wise ways of sustaining a party.

At all events he saved himself from unpopularity.

It is difficult for a man who views both hunting and shooting with languid contempt, who speaks exquisite French, who hates rain like a cat, and who never conceals that he is infinitely bored by everybody around him, to be even tolerated in an English county. But Avillion was more than tolerated, he was almost adored, with the kind of mysterious glory about him which attaches to a Grand Llama or a Veiled Prophet.

A great peer has no longer in England the power and glamour which he possessed in the early days of the century, when he wore his Garter ribbon in his painted coach, whilst his six or eight stately horses drew him home through his country mead; the Reform Bill shattered the great and solid aristocracy which stood up in its solitude against Napoleon as no democracy ever could or ever would stand against anything. But it may be doubted whether the cheapening of nobility by the introduction of trade-bought titles, and the prostrating of ancient races in craven submission to Radical demands, have not injured the English aristocracy more than any Reform Bills could have had power to do. The prince who 'makes himself cheap' digs the grave of all royalty. Yet in a society which already possesses all that wealth, luxury, and indulgence can give it, and which is sensible that it has lost its manners, its dignity, and its distinction, *chic* is the only thing left for it to covet and solicit; and Avillion possessed, and his presence conferred, supreme *chic*, as his exclusiveness was known to be rigid and immutable. When a hostess could murmur, 'You will meet Lord Avillion,' it was as when in the days of Marly and Versailles some châtelaine could say 'le Roy y sera.'

For the individual to unite an occasional sweetness and affability to an habitual distance and mystery is to have captivated the minds of the general. Avillion captivated it thus.

He was in reality everything which an

English county abhors; and yet he contrived to be so admired, wondered at, and speculated on, that no one in his county believed in his faults and almost everyone would have taken his part, right or wrong. He knew it; and it amused him vastly. 'Nothing is easier than to have the verdict of your county in your favour,' he said once with his finest smile. 'Spend a great deal in it, and live a great deal out of it. They don't know much about you, but they all *feel* you agreeably then. If you build a new church you need never enter one, new or old. Nay, even a painted window will get you plenary indulgence for ten years. Why do people ever run their heads against stone walls? You can do just as you like with a little tact. A stained window in a church will buy you the kingdom of heaven on earth. It is so easy to put up a stained window!'

With all his cosmopolitanism, cynicism, and contemptuousness, he had an uneasily conventional side to him. Every Englishman has this; it made Byron marry Miss Milbanke, and Shakespeare leave one of his best beds to his wife; it made Avillion desire to possess the praise of persons whom he scorned, and he had put up more than one stained window by famous artists in the cathedral-town nearest Brakespeare, and had built a whole new church in the small borough which lay at the foot of the hill of Brakespeare, clustered underneath the mighty shadow of its walls and towers, where it had stood as far back as the days of the Rival Roses.

The artists' and architects' bills, though heavy, were no great burden to him, and they prevented the entire body of the clergy of his county ever asking too curiously why Lord Avillion was so much away out of England, and who the pretty unknown women were, who were occasionally seen with him when he was in England, at race-meetings, and at yachting-races.

Even in their decadence and deflorescence the English aristocracy is still a name to conjure with, when those who have it know the rites and measures of the magic. The province is proud of having a great noble, accomplished, rich, and magnificent, in the midst of it, and though malcontents may murmur and begrudge, the majority are attracted by him like the moths by the lamp.

At the same time, Syrlin was at Willowsleigh, and refused the innumerable invitations to great houses which rained on him, on the plea that he required rest and repose. It was rumoured that he was composing a poem or a play, and conjecture ran wild as to his reasons for making a hermitage under the willows and cedars of Surrey.

August followed July, and still found him there, with the world shut out on the other side of his gates. It was generally rumoured that he was writing a tragedy in which he intended to re-appear at the Théâtre Français, or was perhaps translating Shakespeare, to act as Hamlet, Biron, or Romeo in a new reading of those parts. Auriol encouraged these rumours.

'We are only let alone when others all believe that they know what we are about,' he said to Syrlin, with much truth.

For a time carriages flocked up to the inland entrance of his retreat, and canoes and boats of all sorts, undeterred by the warning of 'private water,' crowded to the river-steps of it; but as the occupants of the first saw nothing but a long avenue and a surly porter, and the occupants of the latter found an iron cheval de frise barring the landing-place, all of them, sooner or later, grew tired and did not renew their enterprise.

He, who was at all times disposed to thrust his foot against his throne and push it into space, shivered to atoms, cared nothing for public opinion. He shut himself up in the solitude of Willowsleigh as he was wont to do in that of his tower of St. Germains, partly in extreme resentment against the interference of Beaufront, but more from that melancholy pleasure in its own pain which a forbidden passion enjoys.

'I assure you he is only sulking!' said Auriol to everybody; but Society could not accept so simple an explanation; it does not allow its artists to sulk, it does not allow even its princes to do so; they must be always on the treadmill before its eyes, always going to and fro, always running hither and thither, always conventional, conspicuous, correct, always smiling, bowing, declaring themselves pleased, poor toilers of the purple!

Syrlin wandered like a lover in verse up and down the lonely avenues and grassy glades of his new possession. Every interruption to his own thoughts was unwelcome to him; he was unwilling to have any reminders of his past life or the outer world thrust on him. All the romance of his temperament, all the tenacity of a spoilt child of fortune, and all the strength of a nature which remained singularly unworn and impetuous, were together concentrated on one woman. The famous dictum that absence strengthens great passions is not always nor often true; but it is occasionally true, and it was so with him. His desire to see her again grew in those few weeks of solitude into an overwhelming longing, and his bitterness against her husband grew in intensity with it. To have committed any folly, any insanity, almost any crime, would have been rapture to him, but he restrained his fiery impulses from deference to her.

Love, like every other sentiment and motive of action, has been vulgarised by modern life.

And this Romeo, this Stradella, who had no affinity with modern feelings and modern usages, shrank as the most delicate girl would have shrunk, from letting the electric light of curiosity and comment on the idol of his thoughts. At the white heat of a passion he would have lost every remembrance of the outer world; but in solitude, in reflection, he felt that he would die a hundred deaths before he would let the hem of her garment be soiled through him. Nature had made him utterly void of prudence, bold to folly, and unwise as the generous and courageous temper always is. But in the loneliness of his riverside woods he tried to change his nature; he strove to control and to efface himself, and he suffered in proportion to the strength of his efforts.

He was now in that conventional world which exacts from all men and women the monotony of polished and insincere repression of all emotions, and he felt that he could not for her sake revolt against its tyranny.

He knew that she was a woman never to forgive what should make her the target of that world's arrows. He had hated and scorned conventionality all his life, and now it had its revenge, and opposed to him the smooth impassable wall of its own unchangeability.

To bear a woman across the saddle over the brown plains of Morocco, with hostile javelins and spears darkening the air and bullets whistling past his ear, would have been easy and exquisite to him; but to draw down on her the gross conclusions, the malevolent constructions, the coarse and the mean injuries of the envenomed insipidity of the modern world, would have been intolerable to him.

Auriol, who was sympathetic to him with that kinship of all artistic and poetic temperaments, alone was admitted within the gates of Willowsleigh, and in the hush of the midsummer evening their voices, and the chords of their lutes, echoed through the moonlit, rose-scented, dew-laden air in that voluptuous and melancholy interpretation of the passions which music alone can give.

'You should have been a singer; you would have been greater than I,' said Auriol one night.

'I wish to heaven I had been,' replied Syrlin. 'I wish I had been anything rather than a mime, imitating, and so degrading, the passions and the emotions which I never felt.'

'Oh, my dear Hernani!' cried Auriol, 'have I not known you madly in love a thousand times?'

'In love, perhaps,' said Syrlin with scorn; 'that is not to love.'

The distinction did not seem clear to Auriol; but he understood that it was clear to his friend and he was mute, with that wisdom which sympathy teaches.

So the summer weeks drifted away, and the house at Willowsleigh became beautiful under the changes made in it by its present owner. He believed, he assured himself, that Lady Avillion would, sooner or later, on her return come thither to some fête to which he would be able to attract her, and he pleased himself in endeavouring to anticipate and meet her tastes in every way. The house was late eighteenth century in architecture and decoration, a period conspicuous in England for its offences to taste, but capable of association by French art with much that was charming and graceful in the Louis Seize epoch. It was to a *genre Grand Trianon* worthy of a great queen that he restored it, whilst, as Avillion had surmised, he brought over to it his eighteenth-century pastels and his Gobelins of that time.

'There is only wanting the sun of Versailles,' said Auriol, 'the sun which will soon be wanting all the world over, if steam and smoke increase.'

'Yes, it wants the light,' said Syrlin. 'These shepherds and shepherdesses, these dancers of gavottes and pipers of rondelays, look pale and chilly. Gobelins is always gay, and yet it is always sad, because it tells us of a day that is dead.'

'Oh no, it makes a sunshine of its own

even here, in the rain-mists of the Thames Valley. I am a barbarian, I suppose, but I would sooner have Gobelins on my walls than Flemish or Florentine arazzi. They have such a happy look of the Golden Age about them always.'

'One could have pretty fêtes here,' said Syrlin. 'But the summer will be gone before—'

'Before she will return,' he was about to say, and Auriol understood what was unspoken and asked no questions. His own thoughts were with the young, high-born maiden who was so far above his reach in the esteem of the world, whose heart, nevertheless, he felt was drawn to his.

Syrlin welcomed him whenever he went there with the sincerity of friendship founded on mutual taste and mutual confidences, but even this interference with his thoughts was an irritation to him, although he controlled himself from any betrayal of inhospitable feeling. He liked to be absolutely alone with his memories and his hopes; his life was at a pause. He waited for he knew not what. He had no hope, and yet he vaguely hoped. An expectation which had no definite shape or name filled all his being with its troubled sweetness.

He loved a woman who was as unattainable as the stars; and yet, being a poet at heart and so a dreamer of vain dreams, he believed that his future held the possibility of joy.

A romantic and apparently hopeless passion was the only one which could have had any power to hold him for any length of time; his successes had been too many, his triumphs too easy, for any facile love to have had any lasting place in his imagination; and in an artistic temperament the imagination always plays the larger part in passion, it is at once its root and its flower.

Lady Avillion was a woman of great beauty, of unusual intelligence, and of strong character, whilst her life was one wholly outside the deep emotions and the warmer joy of which existence is capable; but his fancy made her far more than this, clothed her with qualities, beauties, miseries, desires, needs, which never existed in her, and pitied her passionately for sorrows which never were hers. He could have comprehended the horror of a Lucretia, because that kind of chastity was in itself a passion; a strong, savage, sacred thing which chose death sooner than surrender. But the attitude of a woman of rank to whom all unwise or illegitimate sentiment was impossible from traditions of pride and preference of position, was a formalism of which he had no conception. He perceived that the conventionalities, views, habits, and prejudices of her caste and world had entered deeply into her; but he did not realise that they were in truth herself, and no more to be separated from her than the cuticle of her skin or the cartilage of her bones. A nature which by instinct and habit is intolerant of all conventional views and forms can ill comprehend the extent to which these penetrate and pervade a character steeped in them by long usage and custom and tradition. To a man like Syrlin honour meant independence, candour, generosity, freedom from all trammel and dictation: to a woman like Lady Avillion honour meant complete immunity from all weaknesses which could invite or permit injurious comment. These two conceptions of it are as wide asunder as the poles: the one is a law to itself, the other in all its pride is a bondage.

Inspired by all which tortured him, his natural and latent talents reached new developments. '*Sa plume se souvenait d'avoir été une aile,*' and the genius in him which had been but the interpreter of poets, made

him a poet who drew his inspiration from
his own heart alone. Life with him was still
upon the morning side of its meridian, and
he had time before him in which to make
a triumphal poem of it before the shadows
lengthened into afternoon. He was unhappy,
but his unhappiness was of that kind which
at once stimulates and spiritualises the mind
of a man of genius, and in the desire for
solitude which it creates, elevates and
strengthens him. Syrlin had never before
been a poet in expression, but under the
stimulus and sting of a vehement and almost
hopeless passion he became so. These long
and solitary weeks, with no companionship
save at intervals that of Auriol, were fruitful
of deep thought and melodious harmonies.
He was young, he had a wide future before
him; he had those powers which are ductile
as clay in the hands of the sculptor; great
ambitions arose in him like those which had
shed their gorgeous rays upon his dreamy
boyhood; he felt that he had in him those
forces which are obedient ministers to the
man of genius when he knows how to remain
their master and not become their slave. All
the passion and pain and futile aspirations
which were in him he poured out into his

first lyric and dramatic composition, which grew from a mere sketch into a serious and lofty creation, play and poem in one. The poetic temperament seeks instinctively refuge and solace in artistic expression ; and not wrongly have the songs of the wild swan dying amidst the frozen rushes been taken as emblem and epitome of the sufferings of the poet.

He thought of her by day and by night, waking and sleeping, dreaming of some vague and ineffable future, intangible as the glories of sunrise, and repeating to himself in the words of his favourite poem :

> Non !—Je reviendrai maître de ma pensée
> Et de mon souvenir ;
> Et lorsque enfin sera toute trace effacée
> Qui pourrait les ternir,
> A ses pieds, attendant que son regard y tombe,
> Je mettrai quelque jour,
> Comme un pâtre à genoux présente une colombe,
> Mon pur et jeune amour.

It was the desire of the knight to be glorified in his lady's sight and rewarded by his lady's hand, which awakened in him all those dreams of his boyhood which had only slumbered and had never died within him. So had Chastelard dreamed before him, only to find eternal oblivion in the pool of blood beneath the headsman's block.

CHAPTER XLII

THE sovereign of his dreams, worthy or unworthy of them, was, after a few weeks of Aix, passing her time under the slender larches of Marienbad, dividing the attention of the invalided crowds with an empress and two crown-princesses, carrying her fair head haughtily as usual, and professing herself amused, interested, rested, invigorated, charmed. In herself, she was extremely irritated and inexpressibly bored. The days seemed to her of an incredible length, the society of an unutterable vacuity.

Marienbad is one of those places which, in themselves characterless, take the aspect of your own thoughts to you, and become tedious, or refreshing and innocent, according as your own mood be serious or smiling. There is nothing in it of that magic which some scenes possess, of forcing you out of yourself, and into an union of soul with them in their storms or in their sunshine. It gives to you only what you take to it; and as she only took to it irritation, perplexity, and depression, its quiet, sober gaieties, and its level landscape, became to her the *ne plus ultra* of all that was tiresome, uninteresting, and monotonous, from the jaded seekers after health, with their damaged digestions, to the mathematically regular walks and drives in the monotonous plantations.

'What would the Greeks have thought of us?' she said to a friend. 'What would the Greeks have said to us? Eating and drinking so much through ten months of the year, that we are obliged to spend the other two months virtually in a hospital. The hospital has green walks and a fine band, but it is none the less a hospital. In classic times the *vomitorium* was at the end of the table: we have it at the end of the season. With all our gourmandise, and our hypochondria, and our endless fuss and fever over ourselves, all will finish in a gulf of retributive Socialism, as a factory is whirled down under a cone of rotatory wind!'

With not more vanity than every charming woman possesses, she had been conscious of her successes and convinced of her utility, and sometimes amused if oftener wearied by her world; but since she had known Syrlin, all this had changed.

There are sometimes single words which, like the touch of a disenchanting wand, make the whole palace of our views and feelings crumble uselessly in a moment. Words of Syrlin's had been like this with her. Before the sincerity, the ardour, and the hatred of formalities and conventionalities which vibrated with so much force in every utterance of his, the formalism and insincerity of her own life, and that which was always around her, had been revealed to her. She shut her eyes to the fact, but it influenced her none the less.

'If we were only even amused,' she thought; 'amused as the Venetians were in Goldoni's days, or the Parisians in Molière's! It might be selfish, it might be puerile, it might be even base; but it would be real, it would be excusable. As it is, we are intolerably wearied by a conventional life, from which we cannot escape because it is an *engrenage* into which we have entered. And our duties, our occupations, are as fictitious as our pleasures, and as tedious. Who is to alter it all?'

When social interests and mental exertions which have always been ample occupation for us become through any cause insufficient for our amusement and employment, we are conscious of a mutilation, of a loss, as painful as the mutilation or loss of a limb or a faculty. And it was this which Freda Avillion now suffered from, without being sensible of the cause. All those things and people which had hitherto sufficiently filled her life became insufficient to her; what had always appeared to her of supreme importance had shrunk into mere nothingness; and all the views, opinions, pursuits, and interests which had long absorbed and contented her, became to her as little as his neglected playthings appear to a sick child. To her, as to a child, the toys had lost all importance or power to please. The Party playing with primroses and flags, whilst every day they opened their gates a little wider and a little wider to the incoming mud-flood which they abhorred, seemed to her like babies walking backwards into a chalk-pit whilst they strung daisy-chains.

To a woman whose whole character and intelligence have been concentrated on political life, this disillusion was an undoing of her most cherished beliefs, an uprooting of her most consoling sophisms. Contact with the hydra had shown it to her as it was; not a good-humoured though hungry beast, to be patted and propitiated by buns and brass bands, but a devil-fish, risen from unfathomable depths of seas, waiting in its black shapelessness to fasten on and suck under all she held most dear and most sacred.

Whilst she walked beneath the larch trees or conversed with acquaintances at Marienbad, her mind was filled with these disturbed and unsatisfactory thoughts. Her husband's interview with her also had left an indelible and distasteful impression on her mind. It had been altogether unlike Avillion, either to retract or to apologise; altogether unlike him to confess himself in error and withdraw from a position already taken up by him. All imperious natures are touched by submission and all generous natures are won by generosity; hers had been so, for the moment, at his unusual candour and humility. But on reflection, these had worn a little more doubtful aspect to her; she began to reconsider them, and so little were they in accord with Avillion's character, that she ended in being distrustful of and alarmed by them. They had been assumed to mislead her, and they had done so at the first, but they did not do so long.

He wished her to compromise herself; she began to realise this, strange as it seemed in a man who made the only sacrifices he ever made in his egotistical life for the sake of maintaining an appearance of entire harmony with her. And at the perception of his real drift, all the hauteur of her nature was aroused, and with it all the indignation of a woman who knew herself entirely blameless.

'He shall not have his wishes gratified then!' she said to herself. Compromised! She! Almost the only living woman who closed her doors to those popular *pêches à quinze sous*, who were passed everywhere else because they lay in a gilded basket or had been patted by a prince's hand. She would not have forfeited the power to look coldly over the heads of such people, to calmly ignore the 'American set,' to give even royal hosts to understand that she did not care to meet in their circles certain persons who had no passport there except a pretty face, to stand firmly, if almost alone, against the invasion of a popularity and a plutocracy begotten out of rottenness like a toadstool; she would not have forfeited her power to do this for any consideration which could have been offered to her. Higher motives might or might not be her guiding star, but this sense was ever present with her, that nothing

on earth could or should ever tempt her to
do the smallest thing that would ever place it
in the power of these women to say that she
was even as they were.

The world is very good-natured to
'naughty people' if they are pleasant or pretty
people likewise; but she, regardless of being
out of the fashion, had always viewed this kind
of levity with dislike and treated it with
rigorous exclusion, not so much as a matter
of virtue, as a matter of taste. The idea
suggested by Avillion's words, that these very
people should perhaps already think that they
had it in their power to make a jest of her,
was intolerable to her. It made a tinge of
impatience and anger stir in her even against
Syrlin himself, though she was conscious of
the ingratitude of it. In all her admiring
remembrance of his action, she could not help
wishing that it had been less dramatic, less
public, less sensational, to use the cant word
of the hour. It had roused all her best and
warmest feelings; it had touched her to that
delight in a man's courage which courageous
women feel; no knight plunging into the
sulphurous flames of a dragon's jaws could
have been more admirable in his lady's eyes
than he was in hers. And yet, such ingrates,

and so poor of spirit, does the world render us, that she resented the heroic brilliancy of the exploit. To a person whose nature is by instinct noble, to be conscious of motives which are not noble, not courageous, not candid, is a very distinct humiliation, and she was humiliated by the consciousness of her own. All that was best in her impelled her to express and testify her admiration and gratitude for the man who had the right to both; but the habits of the world, the dislike of comment, the tenacity of position, all equally impelled her to conceal them.

When she heard of his purchase of the estate of Willowsleigh, she was, or persuaded herself to believe that she was, angered at so marked and open a selection of residence in a country with which he had no affinity, and in which he was wholly an alien.

'Syrlin living in England! He is as much at home as a nightingale in a cellar!' said Beaufront, whom she saw in Vienna when he went there in the race-time. She was conscious that he looked at her with a scrutiny which offended her, she perceived that in his own mind he associated her with that sudden selection of residence.

'I suppose it is a caprice,' she said with

indifference. 'Artists are always having strange fancies, but they seldom last long. As soon as the place is in order, he will probably have it put up for sale.'

'Did you know anything of his intention? The river fogs will ruin his voice. You might have dissuaded him.'

'I had not the slightest knowledge of his intentions; I am not an estate-agent. Certainly I should have told him it would be better not to commit such a folly. Why did not you? You were in London.'

'I did tell him. But he is *très entêté*; he never can be persuaded or convinced. He is very much changed, disagreeably changed of late, grown quite morose.'

'I should not suppose he was ever remarkable for sweetness of temper,' replied his cousin with impatience. 'It is an unpoetic quality which he would not be likely to possess, and I should not think that the fogs of the Thames Valley will give it him?'

'You are not very grateful, Freda,' said Beaufront unwisely, irritated by the superciliousness of her tone.

'Grateful!' she repeated, as people repeat a word who are not at all sure what they wish to reply. 'On the contrary, I am fully sensible of all I owe to your friend's opportune presence and courage. But I think it would have been better taste in him not to emphasise his claim to it by so very odd a proceeding as buying a property in a country with which he has nothing in common, and where, as you sensibly say, the fogs will probably ruin his voice. If he had bought a palace in Morocco amongst his Moors and his Arabs, it would have been much more in his rôle.'

'He has his mother's house in Morocco,' said Beaufront with unreasonable annoyance, 'and I quite agree with you that it would be much better for him to go to it. Amongst barbarous Moors the taking of life is certainly not much thought of, but on the other hand, the saving of life is esteemed a fine thing, at least by the owners of the life. In Morocco, if he had done for a woman what he did for you, all the tribe would have been his clansmen, all their possessions would have been as his, all their horses and weapons would have been at his service; whereas we—we and you—in our frigid, narrow, odious, contemptible civilisation, are only half ashamed of it, and are wholly annoyed that anyone or anything should have laid us open to having newspaper paragraphs written about us,'

'It is easy for Arabs and Moors to be amiable; they have no newspapers!'

'They are not amiable, they are semi-savages; but they have, in some things, better instincts than we. We are so bound and chilled by our own interest, and the consideration of what others will say of us, that we have become incapable of any spontaneous warmth of feeling.'

'Do you approve of spontaneous warmth of feeling?' said his cousin, with her most indifferent expression. 'It is extremely inconvenient sometimes; not to say *inconvenant*. Would you have liked me to have pinned a ribbon off my gown on to your friend's coat in Piccadilly? It would have pleased the mob. They resemble your Arabs in some respects.'

Beaufront very nearly swore.

'You are the most irritating woman who exists, sometimes!' he said with great anger.

'You have often told me so,' said Freda tranquilly. 'I have no intention of irritating anybody.'

'You succeed admirably, without intention!'

'My dear Ralph, you are always so easily irritated. If I had pinned on that ribbon, the mob might have been pleased, but you would not have been pleased, nor any of our people.'

'How can you talk that rubbish about ribbons? You are a very cold nature, Freda.'

'Am I? It is fortunate for me.'

'I never know what you are nowadays,' said Beaufront, with depression and a sense of ill-treatment.

'I suppose you go back soon?' he inquired abruptly.

'One must. One must have people in October.'

'Will you invite Syrlin?'

A flush of anger passed over her countenance; the question struck her as extremely insolent and offensively curious.

'Certainly!' she replied, in a tone intended to close the conversation.

'That is more condescension than I expected from you,' said Beaufront, 'for a madman who drove you ten yards bareheaded, and was cheered by the mob! You can't seriously mean to ask him amongst sane and decent people, who would rather lose their heads than their hats, and only blandly lend their carriages to mobs on polling-days!'

'They have not much in their heads to lose, most of them,' said Lady Avillion coldly. 'And I think they are always careful to lend their *old* carriages.'

She perceived her cousin's desire to question, advise, and censure her; and she did not choose that he should do any one of the three.

He was unreasonable and he knew it. A few weeks before he had quarrelled with Syrlin for having attracted attention to his cousin's name; and he was now nearly quarrelling with her for an indifference to Syrlin which was the most desirable sentiment she could harbour. Nothing would have displeased him more, or seemed more deplorable, than any warmth of feeling in her in the matter, and yet he felt now that she was unworthy, and shallow, and callous, to be thus untouched by so great a service rendered to her.

'A woman of the world has no real feeling in her,' he thought bitterly. 'She could not live the life of the world if she had. She is always occupied with externals. Infinite trivialities seem to her the essence of existence, and a question of precedence or a breach of etiquette has all creation hanging on it for her. How could he ever dream of attaching himself to her! He might as well hope for response from one of her own orchids. I told him long ago what women like this were, and he would not understand; he would run blindfold against a marble wall!'

Beaufront, who beneath his cynicism had the warmest and most capacious heart where his friends were concerned, had a sincere affection for Syrlin, and was infinitely distressed at a situation out of which no good could come for anyone, as far as he himself could see or foresee. He could not have wished that his cousin should be more impressionable, but it angered him to find in her no admiration, no appreciation, no sentiment of any kind towards a man who had done so much for her.

'Why,' he thought, 'why are the women we most love always those on whom both passion and constancy are altogether wasted—altogether slighted and misunderstood?'

CHAPTER XLIII

THAT Consuelo Laurence could, after refusing himself, continue her usual mode of life, could care to carry her graceful person from one country-house to another, could amuse herself with dressing five times a day, could smile serenely on all who approached her, and wander with elasticity and equanimity through rose-gardens in England, and over heather-covered hills in Scotland, seemed to him monstrous.

'Externals are all that women care for,' thought Beaufront. 'They love all that daily ceremony, that hourly hypocrisy, that ceaseless change of dress, that incessant make-believe to be amused, to be charmed, to be cordial, to be devoted, which constitutes the routine of society; all the network of small intrigue is a labyrinth of delight to them; they are never so happy as when they are smiling on a person they hate for some trivial end that they conceive to be paramount, and they are incapable of any sorrow which cannot be consoled by the knowledge that they are the best-dressed women in the circle at Sandringham. The *infiniment petit* is their paradise, and all their emotions are subordinate to the facts that their jewel-case should travel safely, and that their gowns are wholly beyond all rivalry!'

Beaufront was restless and ill at ease. Nothing went with his friends as he wished. Consuelo Laurence had left London unmoved in her decision, and had, he rashly concluded, neither tenderness towards him nor belief in his word; she was flitting from one great house to another, in her usual fashion, coveted and complimented in all, continuing in her series of visits that life of the world to which she declared herself an alien, but to which she was as entirely suited as a swan to the silvery smoothness of an artificial lake.

He had gone out of England himself in pique against her, and in a sincere pain and anxiety for his cousin. He was tired of the routine of the season and post season. His world went with him wherever he turned his steps. The Duke of Beaufront could arrive nowhere unobserved, unchronicled. He sighed impatiently for the days when Ralph Fitzurse had made involuntarily protracted sojourns for want of money to pay his bill at the same hotels where now His Grace of Beaufront was met with a servility and adulation which seemed to him sickening and detestable.

'Seven years ago you were afraid to give me a cigar and a glass of seltzer on credit,' he said to an obsequious innkeeper, who walked backwards to usher him into a grand suite of apartments at Wiesbaden.

'O, most high! if I had then known—' murmured the man, overwhelmed with confusion and contrition.

Beaufront gave a little hard curt laugh.

'Never mind; you judged according to your light,' he said to the discomfited Boniface.

Of course, like this man, if the world could have been 'in the know,' as the slang of sport phrases it, it would not have made the mistake of slighting and avoiding him. It was natural enough, reasonable enough, no doubt.

The world can only measure, roughly and readily, by such measurements as these. A man without money is a marked man to it, because money is its handiest and readiest gauge, not of actual worth indeed, but of that prosperity, that utility to others, which are its favoured and favourite qualities. The man himself, so long as he remains honest, is just as good and as worthy of esteem, whether he be worth nothing financially, or be worth millions. But the world in general has no time or temper to explore his qualities, moral or mental; it judges him roughly by the test which is of most use to itself and most visible and most easily computed, that of his monetary means.

Beaufront knew human nature too well to complain of this, and yet he never ceased to chafe at it. He despised everybody who paid court to him, and on his naturally warm-hearted and generous character this kind of cynicism produced anger and depression. Where his cousin, in similar circumstances, would have smiled at the time-serving, he was filled by it with impatience and disgust and distress. At this moment when, wisely or unwisely, the rejection of his offer had made him seriously unhappy, he told himself that it was wholly useless to be the lord of many lands and many houses, if he could not be sure of a single heart which beat with an undivided and disinterested attachment towards himself. It might be sentiment, he told himself, but sentiment is after all the summer of our lives.

'Beau is as cross as a bear,' said the acquaintances who encountered him at the various pleasure-places to which Englishmen love to resort to lighten their lives and purses, and none of them had any patience with a man who so capriciously and ungraciously quarrelled with the fine fortunes on which he had entered, and the sunshine of fate in which he could bask at his will.

Once, walking home from the Kursaal of Homburg through the woods in a moonlight night, the idea occurred to him to write his offer once more to Consuelo Laurence. Beaufront, like many men, was not an accomplished writer ; he needed the animation of companionship to spur on his thoughts to expression. When he wrote he was shy with a sense that those who would read would laugh at him. But this night he reflected again and again on what he wanted to say, and when he reached his temporary abode he sat down beside an open window through which the wind rustled as it came over the pines, and the moon shone from her place over the Taunus mountains, and he did for once write as he could, when strongly moved, speak, earnestly, forcibly, and with no stint of expression. He said to her again on paper what he had said in her house in Wilton Street; and it seemed to him that it acquired irresistible weight and proven sincerity in being thus written clearly and solemnly in the stillness and solitude of night.

'If that do not fetch her, I will never ask her again, if I die for it,' he thought as he walked out once more and himself posted the letter, while the town slept under the stars, and the fragrance of the surrounding forests filled the air with that *Mondnacht* which has inspired Schumann with one of his most beautiful themes.

He awaited the reply with impatience and a strength of desire which surprised himself. Why should he all of a sudden so intensely wish to associate with his own a life which had such deep shadows on it, and which was already past the years of youth? He could not have said, except that he felt with her what Napoleon felt with Josephine, profound serenity and the sense of that intuitive companionship which needs no words. Sympathy is not necessarily love, and love in the sense of passion may exist without it; but it is the next best thing to it, and may even surpass and supplant it. He waited with intense impatience, and an amount of hope which was almost certainty that her answer would be in the affirmative. She could not doubt his sincerity, his deliberate choice, his unalterable wish to bestow on her all that he had in his gift, now that in black and white he had renewed his offer to her. Spoken words may be the airy flighty children of a second's impulse, but written words are surely the weighed and matured offspring of a deeply rooted conviction. As such he believed that his must speak to her.

When on the sixth morning from the night on which he had posted his letter he recognised her writing on an envelope bearing a Scottish postmark, he tore it open with fingers which trembled as they would assuredly never have done holding sword or revolver in a life-and-death combat.

Consuelo Laurence wrote from Strathniel, a hunting place in the Western Highlands belonging to the Marquess of Firth. The words were few, but they left no doubt as to their finality and force.

'Why will you torment yourself and me?' she said with no preliminary or prefix. 'I have never doubted your sincerity or your nobility; how could I do so in the face of such proofs of both as you are willing to give me? What I do not, cannot, never shall believe in is, that you are either wise or right in thus addressing me, or that you would not ere long regret the consequences to yourself if I answered you as you now desire. You are the most generous, the most trustful of all men; but I will neither abuse your generosity nor strain your trust. The future will give you fairer things than those that a *femme tarée* could bring to you. You only distress me uselessly and unspeakably by opening afresh a subject which I had thought was closed for ever between us. I am not so utterly unworthy of your offer as to accept it. I am sincerely and unalterably your friend, but as sincerely and unalterably I tell you that I shall never be more than that. God bless you, dear.'

It was signed Consuelo, and the pale paper on which it was written brought with it that faint sweet perfume of lime flowers which was especially her favourite.

Beaufront grew very pale as he read it, and the faint perfume of the paper seemed to him like the scent of flowers which lie on a grave.

'She does not care, or she could not reason so coldly,' he thought bitterly, and yet as he read and re-read the lines, he felt that she did care, and the rough impatient anger which had been in his heart against her was merged in the unwilling admiration which the generosity of his nature could not refuse to the generosity of hers.

'I can never ask her again,' he had said, and yet he knew that he would leave no stone unturned until he should conquer her decision and convince her that the happiness of his future lay in her hands, and in those of no other.

A week or two later Beaufront went where his cousin was, under the larch woods of the Bohemian bath. She was not very glad to see him, and he perceived it.

'You will be bored to death here, Ralph,' she said to him on the day of his arrival.

'I have no doubt of it,' replied Beaufront. 'I am bored in a great many places, but I survive it. I wish we were like the fire-flies and carried our own illumination about with us independent of atmosphere; but we don't.'

'Even fire-flies cannot sparkle in bad weather,' said Freda. 'Everything is dependent on something else.'

'Melancholy truth, it is! But I never knew you admitted it.'

'I always admit a fact.'

'Not surely when it goes against your theories.'

'Oh! I am not wedded to any theories. Nothing seems to me very clearly established. Probabilities, possibilities, are all we really reach.'

'Good heavens! What becomes of the Tory party?'

'The Tory party wants neither theories nor facts; it only asks for catchwords and formulas, and those borrowed clothes which Sir Robert Peel was so epigrammatically accused of stealing when the Whigs were bathing.'

She spoke rather wearily than jestingly, and as he looked at her, the brilliant and proud beauty of her face seemed to him dimmed and shadowed by a look of care.

'You have seen the Tory toy face to face, haven't you?' he said gravely, 'and you realise now, that it is not a clumsy good-humoured pet to be quieted with sugar and cream, but a many-headed ravenous bull-dog that wants blood and reeks of offal. It is not a beast to be led about by primrose-chains, and soothed by the tinkling of ladies' guitars and violins. What do you think now?'

'Do not let us talk of it.'

'You wish to forget that scene? That I can quite understand. But if it has shown you the vanity of your political illusions, it will not have been lived through in vain.'

'Are they all illusions? We are at least sincere in them.'

'The ladies of the Fronde were sincere also in their way, yet they did great mischief.'

'There is no parallel. We are constitutionalists, not Frondeuses.'

'Constitutionalists? Yet you have approved and passed the most Radical measure of the century; the clothes which the Tories have not only borrowed but stretched to splitting.'

She was silent, absently drawing with the ferule of her tall walking stick, lines and figures on the sand of the alley where they were seated.

'I admit,' she said gravely after a while, 'I admit that the hopelessness of ever reconciling the mob and the State seems great to me since that day. I realised then that we are living over a volcano, which I used to think a very absurd hyperbole.'

Abruptly he put before her the letter of Consuelo Laurence.

'Read that,' he said curtly. 'Tell me what you think now of the writer.'

She read it very slowly, weighing and studying every phrase. Then she folded it up and gave it back to him.

'I think she loves you,' she said simply.

The colour rose hotly over his face. He was strongly moved at this unlooked-for testimony.

'Where can you possibly see that? The letter is as cold as ice.'

'Oh no. It is far from cold. It is the sort of letter that a woman would write with a breaking heart. I have always believed Mrs. Laurence a scheming adventuress, who entangled you in every way; I think now that I was mistaken.'

'Thank you, dear,'

Beaufront's voice was hoarse with emotion, and his eyes were dim. He put the letter back in the breast pocket of his coat.

'Then if—if I can ever persuade her to reverse her decision, I shall have your acquiescence, your approval? Mind you, I am convinced myself that she does not care. But if by any chance you should judge rightly—if she should indeed care—you would support her amongst our own people, you would say so to the world, you would no longer disapprove my marriage with her?'

'Ah no, excuse me,' she replied with a return to her chilliest, most distant manner. 'I would not accept such a responsibility. I believe the lady does love you, and I make no doubt you will, if you continue to wish it, succeed in overcoming her scruples. But it will be a marriage of which no friend of yours could approve. My opinion of her past relations to you is not in the least changed. I only see that she is a woman, generous enough, perhaps grateful enough, to set aside her own interests, and only consider yours. Such a self-sacrifice is rare, is indeed very fine, but were you to marry her I should be none the less shocked and grieved.'

'I shall marry her,' said Beaufront stubbornly and passionately between his teeth. 'There will be nothing in that to shock you or to grieve you. She is an entirely noble and innocent woman, and if it be true, which I doubt, that she loves me, life will become worth living to me.'

Freda drew a little away from him, with a very cold look in her eyes.

'All London has considered her *entretenue* by you for many years; you will never be able to disprove it.'

'I shall not attempt to disprove it,' said Beaufront sternly. 'Only if any other woman besides yourself says it, or anything like it, I shall thrash her nearest male relative, whoever he be, in the first public place that I meet him in; it will not be said twice.'

'All that kind of thing is gone out,' said Lady Avillion with chill contempt.

'It will come in again then,' said Beaufront, with eloquent brevity. 'And perhaps you will kindly remember that whether Mrs. Laurence never becomes more to me than she is now, or not, I shall expect her always to receive from you and others as much respect when she is spoken of as if she were my wife.'

'Of course you can say no less,' replied his cousin coldly, 'having the views you entertain. I do not think, however, that you will find it easy to bridle peoples' tongues; and I fear that what they will say will be extremely disagreeable to you if it should ever become generally known that you really intend to marry her.'

'I shall be happy to have it known,' said

Beaufront. 'And now let us speak of the matter no more. You might show me a great mark of friendship and confidence, and you decline to do so. There is no more to be said.'

'My dear Ralph,' replied Freda, with a return to her kindly manner, ' you are bent on killing yourself; you cannot expect your relatives to sharpen the knife and buy the laudanum for you.'

What a sad infatuation! she thought, when he had left her and she pursued her own meditations, whilst answering with monosyllables the acquaintances who surrounded her. What an incredible and melancholy thing that a man in his position, free to marry where he would, should pass by youth and innocence and rank and all kinds of fortuitous circumstances, to desire only to raise to all his dignities a woman whose lover he had been for seven years! It was sorcery. It made her sorrowful to think of it. She regretted the momentary impulse in which candour had made her admit to him that she found genuine and generous emotion in the letter he had shown her; she had been for the instant touched by it, and she had spoken unwisely, for her words had let the light in upon him; she was strongly prejudiced against the writer of this letter, and yet could see in it the suggestion, the certitude, of attachment and abnegation.

He read it again, and yet again, when he was alone, and he began to perceive the possibility of a great affection having dictated its cruel sentences.

He was sensible of the under-current of emotion, the motives of self-abnegation, which were underneath the tranquil and controlled phrases. His hardness against her melted away; he saw that in an access of delicacy, of fear of injuring himself, she chose present pain for him and for herself, rather than accept what she believed that he would ultimately regret or repent having given.

CHAPTER XLIV

'I WONDER,' thought Lady Avillion to herself, and then stopped her wonder on the threshold, undefined and unsatisfied even to herself.

She was in one of the carriages of the London and Dover Railway on her return home. It was a rainy day, the inviolate island of the sage and free is not inviting when approached from the Channel; the white cliffs seem a dirty grey, the landscape, such as it is, looks like a smirched and smudged charcoal drawing, the horizon is low and melancholy, the sense of space and of light is wanting, the still life and the figures in the picture are all uninteresting and unlovely. One understands why Englishmen and Englishwomen call leaving England 'getting away.' 'Getting away'; cruel, ungrateful, but expressive words! meaning such a world of relief, of release from boredom long endured, and deliverance rapturously welcomed. The burden of this thraldom fell heavily on her as she was borne through the level lands of Kent. She had never been so sensible of it before. She was a patriotic woman before everything, and she had always maintained, however unfashionable the opinion was, that there was no place like England. But now its extreme ugliness, its crowded monotony, its muddy muddled aspect, struck her painfully.

'And to think the whole world will be all of that pattern unless a comet comes to destroy it!' she thought with a sigh.

She felt a repugnance against her manner of existence, an impatience of it, a heavy sense of its burden and its uselessness.

'We never do anything new,' she thought; 'it is always the same thing, an enormous expenditure, an incessant fatigue, and no one even amused by it.'

It is a feeling of dreariness and ennui which entrance into England often produces on sensitive natures, but it had never before weighed on hers as it did now. The frightfulness of modern civilisation and its concomitants culminates in Cannon Street Junction; short of Leeds or Pittsburgh nothing so completely dreadful exists anywhere, and its intolerable stench and horror seem insupportable after the green quiet fields of Picardy, the mistletoe-crowned trees and cathedral spires of Amiens and Abbeville.

There are no winter studies that surpass in their kind those to be made in the north of France. The orchards are so luxuriant, the low-roofed cottages so smothered in boughs and branches, the beautiful old church spires rise out of such an intricate mass of woodland that, though it is all level or nearly level ground, there is no impression of flatness, but on the contrary the land is full of nooks and corners which it would take the lifetime of a landscape painter to transfer to canvas. It is the popular idea that nothing can be so prosaic as the country between Amiens and Boulogne which we all traverse so often, but it is most untrue. Its villages and farmhouses are so suggestive of homely romance that one wishes they had a George Sand to immortalise them; and the old mills, the old towers, the old homesteads, are buried in a labyrinth of trees which are almost more beautiful in winter than in summer.

'I feel what Persephone felt when she had to go back into the bowels of the earth,' she said to Lady Ilfracombe with a shiver. 'Out there it was so bright, so big, so clear, so full of pretty colour. To think that we are the first nation in the world in so many ways, and yet that we live in darkness like moles, and that everything we touch we make hideous!'

'Everything,' said her sister, 'except perhaps our country-houses.'

'Yes, our country-houses are nice,' said Freda, but she said it without any enthusiasm; the vision of Brakespeare loomed before her mind's eye with its routine of guests, its oppressive ceremonies, its continual hospitalities, its coming and going of utterly indifferent people.

The train she was seated in lumbered heavily on to a blocked line in Cannon Street, and there stood stock still for half an hour, with smoke and steam and oil befouling the autumn air, and dirty rain-storms dismally sweeping over dull platforms, blackened sleepers, iron girders, opaque glass, and running in dusky streams off the helmets and oilskin capes of policemen and the waterproof leathers of luggage.

After a while the blocked line cleared, the train moved on, and the smutty air, the grating noises, the jarring ugliness, made the green fields, the mistletoe-crowned trees, the cathedral spires, so lately passed on the Ligne du Nord, seem like paradise by comparison.

'What an entrance to a capital city!' she murmured as the train oscillated and screamed into the terminus, and the familar countenance of Phillips, Avillion's own man, looked in at the window of her carriage.

'His lordship was afraid there was an accident, my lady; he expected your ladyship this morning,' said the valet, who felt some vague apology for his unusual intrusion amongst her own servants to be necessary.

'I did not know my lord expected me at all,' she replied in some surprise. 'Is he in town then?'

'He is, my lady; he came up this morning,' answered the man, as astonished as she was at such unusual solicitude in his master.

'How very odd!' said Lady Ilfracombe, as they went to their carriages. 'What, Uther in town in October! What can possibly be the attraction?'

'Myself, apparently,' said Freda with an ironical brevity. 'Oh, how hopelessly murky and dingy and ugly it all is here! Did you see that girl with the red kerchief round her head that was driving geese across a field just after Abbeville? How happy that girl is! She has no need to come to Cannon Street. There was her little cottage behind her tucked up in box hedges and apple trees. Those people are ten thousand times nearer a rational and serene life than we are.'

'Humph!' said Lady Ilfracombe dubiously. She was a woman to whom material pleasures were agreeable; she was thinking drowsily and with interest of the good hot tea and warm bath which would await her at home, and the good dinner, with the evening papers aired and cut, and her favourite dry sherry, which she would find afterwards. It was nearly dark, and the rain and fog made their carriages and horses scarcely visible.

'Good night,' said Lady Ilfracombe as she espied her own brougham and made a little run to it through the rain under her footman's umbrella.

'Good night,' said Freda absently, as she waited for hers to draw nearer; then she gave a startled and astonished glance into the gloom, and saw watching her from a little distance the eyes of Syrlin, those great dark Eastern eyes, which were like no others she had ever seen.

He uncovered his head and stood bareheaded in the rain; he did not seek to approach nearer, but as she took her seat in the carriage a bouquet of orchids, looking of a phantom whiteness in the watery gaslight, were cast through the window and fell upon her lap. She drew the glass up rapidly with an impatient gesture, but she had the bouquet in her hand as she got down at Avillion House; and when she reached her bedroom she put the flowers in water in an old white Worcester basket which had been a favourite with her from her childhood.

There was a note from Avillion on her table; it said :

' May I dine with you at nine? I must go out of town again to-morrow. I am so glad to know you have had a safe and pleasant journey. The children are quite well.'

' What can he want with me? ' she thought as she read it. ' Is there some new woman to be called on or invited ? '

That was what such requests as these always meant from him; and a kindly courtesy of any kind always covered some personal desire which he wished to gratify.

' Say " with pleasure " to my lord,' she answered verbally, and felt the opposite of pleasure.

Never in their lives had Avillion come up to town on purpose to see her on a return from any absence; she knew him too well not to know that there was some ulterior end in such a politeness, and yet, her conscience being restless and ill at ease, she had a sense of being the offender against him.

He greeted her with his usual grace, and with more warmth than usual. They dined together in the small oval room, hung with Dutch pictures of the best masters, which it was customary to use as a dining-room *en famille*.

Avillion was charming, and full of good-humour and of agreeable conversation.

'What can he want of me?' she thought a great many times; but the devilled biscuits had closed the dinner before she had discovered.

'You are not looking very well, my dear Freda,' he said with solicitude, scanning her critically. 'I am afraid those waters are not all that is said of them; and I should say you did not want treatment of that sort. You are blessed with such exceptional, such admirable health; your boys inherit it; they are always well. As for me I am more of a wreck than ever. It is my conviction that none of the doctors know in the least what is really the matter with me.'

'You have the *maladie du siècle*. You do

everything that is injurious ; you smoke perpetually, you are never contented with any place, and you never eat a single thing that is wholesome,' thought his wife, but she had long learned not to say so. She politely regretted that his native air and the simple springs of Buxton had not benefited him.

'No one is ever rewarded for doing their duty,' said Avillion with a sigh. 'They say one ought to be seen in one's county, that it is the absenteeism which is playing into the hands of the Radicals ; but it is a frightful *corvée* ; if there was anything approaching to climate in England one might endure it, but when there is snow on Knavesmire and hail at Goodwood, one's duty becomes really beyond one's strength !'

Despite his imaginary diseases and his real dyspepsia he was looking very well and very handsome ; he had the interest of a thing he desired and could not obtain, and the excitement of a part which he had set himself to play. It gratified him to mislead his wife, whose penetration was deemed so acute, and whose intelligence so often displayed itself in the disdain and ridicule of others. Besides this, his habitual indifference had quickened into an active dislike of her. Since the night when she had refused to bend her will to his, a strong animosity, which only needed provocation to become hatred, had taken the place of that cold approval and contentment with which he had before that regarded her. When dinner was ended and she was about to rise, he looked up at her as he lighted his cigarette:

'Would you mind sitting a few moments longer? I am sure you are tired and longing for your own rooms, but I shall not be able to see you in the morning, as I leave town at ten o'clock. I should like to settle about the Brakespeare invitations. You go down to-morrow?'

'Yes: I want to see the children.'

'Naturally. When will you have your first people?'

'Whenever you please.'

'Oh, I never please! It is the most frightful nuisance. But it must be done. You have been away a long time. I think you had better make out the first list now; do you mind?'

'Oh no.'

She was fatigued and depressed. She had a dull sensation of some impending ill; she had returned to her harness; they were gilded and jewelled trappings no doubt, but they were a yoke all the same, and those great dark eyes of Syrlin's, melancholy and luminous, like the eyes in Abd-el-Kader's portraits, haunted her.

Avillion had taken the pencil off his watch-chain, and was writing the names on the back of his menu-card.

He read them out as he wrote them down, and she acquiesced in the selection absently, scarcely listening to the titles she knew so horribly well; how small and how tedious it was, that 'great world!'

'The Duchess de Charolois,' read Avillion, towards the close of his long list which he had scribbled and erased half a dozen times.

'I do not know her,' said Freda with a slight surprise. 'Do you?'

'I have that honour, since I have met her at Lillieswood and Clouds. You will like her; she is as chilly as a *sorbet*; she is passing through town; she is at her sister's, Lady Lanark's. You know Lady Lanark well enough. You might waive ceremony for once, and call to-morrow?'

'I might,' said Freda, in a tone which implied 'I shall not.'

'I have invited her, but of course she

waits for you,' said Avillion with a little irritation.

'I suppose she does. Society is emancipated, but it still keeps a few prejudices; it still expects the woman of the house to invite her women.'

'Of course you must write to her.'

'When I do not know her!'

'You will invite her with Lady Lanark. If you call it will be better.'

'*Vous y tenez beaucoup?*' said his wife with a slight smile.

'I admire her,' said Avillion calmly, not to be put out of countenance by such a trifle, 'and she has been the fashion since the last Drawing-room.'

Freda said nothing, but wrote down in her note-book: 'to invite Lady Lanark and Mme. de Charolois.'

'Now for the men,' said Avillion, seeing this point was gained.

'You need not consult me about them,' said his wife.

'Oh, it is always best to think them over; a house party must be a symphony, *tempo allegro*, or it is a discord in G sharp and B flat.'

And he went through a list of male

guests, all popular, pleasant, and distinguished persons.

'I wish to have Syrlin, but I am shy about asking him,' he said, looking suddenly at her with that frank expression in his eyes which with him always denoted an intention of duplicity. 'I wish to see him at Brakespeare most especially. Do you think he would come?'

'I cannot say,' replied Freda.

'You know of course he has established himself here? A mistake, I should say, but they tell me he has made the place beautiful. What can possibly lead him to spoil his voice with Thames fogs—'

'I saw it in the papers,' replied Freda in the same tone.

'Ah, in the papers; they tattle about everything. Do you think I may venture to invite him? I wish to make amends to him; will he take it in the right spirit?'

She was silent; Avillion had an exquisite skill in placing others in a dilemma, and shifting a false position from his own shoulders on to theirs. He enjoyed the sense that his wife was profoundly embarrassed, and had for the moment lost her serenity and self-command; she did not look towards him, and the colour in her face changed rapidly. She hesitated a moment longer, then said with no more candour than his own:

'If you are actuated by such amiable feelings, there can be no reason why you should not give expression to them. I do not suppose M. Syrlin will accept, but you can certainly invite him.'

'You are quite sure it will be agreeable to you?' said Avillion with a smile.

'It cannot be otherwise,' she replied with more of her old courage. 'It cannot be otherwise,—to me. Is that all? I am fatigued from my journey; if you have nothing more to ask me I will go to my rooms.'

'A thousand thanks,' said Avillion sweetly, as he rose from the dinner table and opened the door for her. 'A thousand thanks. You should take a little chloral. Believe me there is nothing so good as chloral when one's nerves have been jarred. You look, indeed, very tired; do try it. Good night.'

He went back to his seat, and lighted another cigarette, and smiled.

Her perceptions were very quick, and Avillion's insistence that she should invite Mme. de Charolois had indicated to her the drift of his unusual amiability. She began to suspect that all that apparent candour which had impressed her before her departure for the baths had been only a comedy. She had been really touched by it, and she now knew that she had been duped.

That knowledge is irritating to everyone, and to a woman of fine intelligence and penetration is acutely mortifying.

She went to her own apartments with an uneasy and disgusted oppression upon her as if she had tasted some bitter and unwholesome thing.

'I am to ask Mme. de Charolois, and he in return will invite my friend!' she thought bitterly. 'We could not be more completely in keeping with the "modern tone," more completely in conformity with the "give ·and take" of recognised marital compensation!'

It humiliated her in her own eyes. She had, in all these past years, been blind and deaf to all her husband's very open offences out of wisdom, a sense of dignity, a supreme indifference. But she had been so with a clear conscience, neither needing nor asking any similar indulgence in return. Now it seemed to her as if her forbearance were ignominious, and wore the servile aspect of a dishonourable pact. It was precisely what Avillion desired her to feel.

The light of some wax candles was shining on the china basket of orchids, and the flowers caught her eyes. How had the giver of them known that she was to reach town that evening? She felt the charm of that haunting presence, of that romantic devotion, but they seemed dwarfed, discoloured, and disfigured to her. Avillion approved of them, and saw in them only a convenient and opportune instrument for his own use!

Avillion had proposed to her, in veiled words indeed, but unmistakably, one of those amiable barters which go so far to make married life endurable, but which in others had always seemed to her worthy only of such sovereign contempt. Any form of cowardice was more odious than any sin in her sight, and she felt that she had been cowardly. Understanding, or perhaps more truly speaking divining, a covert insolence in the tone of Avillion's courteous and affable words, she seemed to herself to have lost the power to resist it. Her conscience was quite clear, she had done nothing and said nothing which the most fastidious opinion could blame; *and yet* she was lowered in her own esteem.

She slept ill and awoke little refreshed.
With the morning came the usual formid-

able array of letters, notes, telegrams, and business of all sorts which await, like Nemesis, any length of absence.

The forenoon was wholly occupied with them. At one o'clock they brought her Syrlin's card. She hesitated a little while, then said more peremptorily than was necessary:

'Tell the porter to say that I can receive no one; no one, except members of my own family. I am very much occupied and I leave town to-night.'

When the message was beyond recall she regretted it; the man who had saved her from the mob deserved better than to be turned from her gates.

She knew it, and wrote a few words on a card:

'I regretted that I could not receive you. I leave town directly for Brakespeare, where Lord Avillion hopes, like myself, to see you next week. You will hear from him in the course of the day.'

She addressed it to Syrlin at Willowsleigh.

She did not drive out, for she felt an unacknowledged unwillingness to meet him, as she might do, in the streets.

'You want more secretaries than a Prime

Minister!' said her sister, who came in after luncheon.

'There is so much that secretaries cannot do for us. Who can write our condolences for us or our congratulations? Women of the world are much more really hard-worked than any public man,' said Freda. 'What news is there? I have seen no one.'

'There is not very much just now. One or two bye-elections, as you know: political people attach too much importance to them. They are a kind of weather-gauge certainly, but they do not always point the true way. They say we are to have an autumn session, but I do not believe it. It is such a comfort when the House is up and the Government can go on quietly without all that screaming.'

'Admirable comment upon the Constitution and the Electoral system!'

'I saw your saviour outside your gate,' said Lady Ilfracombe with an unpleasant derision in her voice. 'Do you keep him outside? It is not very grateful.'

'If I receive one person I must receive a hundred, and I have really no time for them,' said Freda with impatience: she was conscious of the unworthiness of the reply.

'Still—Syrlin!' said her sister, 'your

knight, your hero! After all he did you a great service, even if the manner of it was too sensational to be to our taste.'

'There was not much choice of manner,' said Freda curtly. 'We had to get through the mob as we could. Pray do not talk of it. It has brought most unpleasantly home to me the fallacy and futility of all our ideas of government.'

'What do you mean by that?' asked Lady Ilfracombe scandalised.

'What I say. It is not with bunches of primroses and long-winded speeches that we shall kill that hydra which I have seen face to face, and which has only crawled back into its hole to bide its time.'

'Education—' began her sister feebly.

'Education! Education, even if it could be given, which is impossible, would merely make them able to perceive that Socialism is their only useful gospel. Do you suppose that any education can reconcile the hungry man to seeing the dinner tables spread as he looks through the windows of the rich?'

'I never believed that I should live to hear *you* defend Socialism!' cried Lady Ilfracombe with a woman's inconsequence.

'I no more defend Socialism than I defend

the sea when it tears down the esplanade wall at Brighton or Hastings. I only recognise blind overwhelming forces which are beyond our control.'

'Syrlin makes you say all this!'

'Not at all,' said Lady Avillion with a flash of anger. 'I have always been colour-blind; and now I have seen one colour at least plainly enough, and it is blood-red. All Europe will be drowned in that colour one day, for the armies will not for ever consent to ride down and shoot down their fellows.'

'Good heavens!' said her sister faintly, 'what would Lord Greatorex say?'

'Lord Greatorex thinks so in his own private thoughts, or I am much mistaken in the degree of his intellect. He must know very well that he and his policies are only stop gaps, like the rubble and stones which help to fill up the sea-wall at Brighton or Hastings.'

'I hope you will not say this to him or—or—generally!' said Helena Ilfracombe nervously.

Freda laughed a little with a certain bitterness.

'Oh no, I will not disturb the formulas in which I have been bred. One cannot desert one's flag in a day of danger, even if one has realised that it is only calico and tinsel, stuck in the nerveless hand of a lay figure. Let us speak of other things. Have you seen Ina lately? It is so irritating that nothing will induce her to favour Lord Woodbridge, and he so devoted, so persevering, so constant.'

CHAPTER XLV

On leaving England Freda had confided the chaperonage of the girl to her younger sister, Lady Hendon, and had said a few words of warning as to Ina's dangerous imaginative tendency to admire the wrong people, and given other similar directions usual in such cases. But neither her heart nor her mind was very much in the matter, and her sister, who was occupied with her own affairs of sentiment, did not greatly attend; she thought she did all that was necessary in keeping Ina in her own houses or taking her wherever she went herself. Besides, Lady Hendon had quite concluded in her own mind that the child would sooner or later accept Lord Woodbridge, and did not think that a little preliminary flirtation was of any consequence at all.

Lady Hendon liked having artists about her, herself; they were fresh and droll, and helped to pass the time in country-houses; but she never attached any serious import to them; she would as soon have thought the parrots in the conservatories or the lacqueys in the antechambers dangerous to the peace of the realm as have supposed that the artists let loose on society would ever marry into it.

We lived in a decadence, and things were topsy-turvy, and it was the fashion to have all these people about, washed and clothed, and with their hair cut, but no real harm ever came of it; they were made much of whilst their vogue lasted, and when it was over they went back into the obscurity they had come from, and married amongst themselves, and gave lessons—retired lions always gave lessons—that was the view she took of it. .

Up to this time Auriol had never whispered a word of his feelings to Ina's ear; only in the language of music had the secret of his presumptuous attachment betrayed itself. The girl, unversed in all the experiences of the passions, continually doubted the truth of her own intuitions, and reproached herself for vanity in fancying that this sweet singer saw anything more in her than in the hundreds of young girls who passed before him in society.

But pure chance brought them that autumn together in a forest lodge of the Western Highlands, where a great sporting party was assembled, and whither Lady Hendon took her charge. Auriol, who abhorred sport, passed all his time with the women of the party, rowing on the loch, strolling through the heather, and making melody on rainy days in the music-room, which was placed in a grey romantic tower overhanging the lake water, and fronting bold, purple, misty mountains.

In such a scene, thrown day after day into the society of this young high-born maiden, to whom his heart was drawn, playing over to her old, sweet, forgotten scores, he would have been more than mortal if some expression of his feelings had never escaped him clear enough to reveal them unmistakably even to the inexperienced and frightened ear of Ina d'Esterre.

In a few days' time she was carried away by her temporary chaperon to other Scottish palaces of sport and pleasure; but when she went she took with her, for the first time, the unequivocal, undoubted consciousness of Auriol's love for her; and in her valiant young breast, brave despite its hesitancy and shyness, there grew up a firm and courageous resolve, that come what might she would listen to no other.

She knew that to all her people it would

be anathema maranatha that she should even dream of him; that it would be insanity and worse in their eyes that she should ever have listened for an instant to such a declaration; but she was strong of will and independent in opinion despite her gentleness; she had thought and reflected on things beyond her years, and she had a calm though unspoken indifference to all those laws of caste and conventionality which were the evangel of all those who had surrounded and educated her.

'You are an anarchist, Ina!' Beaufront had said to her once at Heronsmere with much amusement and approval; and she had smiled.

'No, I am not that,' she had answered very seriously. 'But I do think that many things do not matter much to which Aunt Freda attaches vital importance.'

'You had better not tell her so,' Beaufront had said. 'She does not like contradiction.'

'Oh no; I should never contradict her,' the girl had replied submissively; but she had added, 'only, you know, if I were quite sure that they did not matter, no one would ever make me say that they did.'

'Bravo!' Beaufront had said with admiration, careless of what rebellious spirit he might encourage.

So that when Ina d'Esterre, for one instant before her departure, left her hand in Auriol's as they bent their heads over some manuscript minuet scores, and murmured back in answer to his nervous and impassioned avowals, 'If you do really care, I will be true to you, no matter what they say,' she meant the words in their very fullest meaning, and had given a pledge which she had not only the wish but the will to keep.

'We need not stay in England if they would be so ashamed,' she thought as she was driven through the falling rain and the lonely Highland hills from one ducal lodge to another. 'We could live in Dresden, or Baireuth, or Rome; I do not care the least about the life they lead here, and all they talk about, and all they think so priceless and so indispensable. It is only art that matters, and being true, and finding one's own happiness in simple things. With all their fuss, and pomp, and haste, and all their stereotyped phrases, they are not really happy; they do not even know what happiness means.'

And her cheeks grew warm, and she closed her eyes to shut out the grey cold Scotch landscape, and she let her thoughts wander to visions of a possible happiness for herself in some far, very far, away future; in some dim old German town amongst cuckoo-haunted pinewoods, or in some white Italian city on a shining sunlit plain.

She had given her future away in a manner which would make her an outcast from all her own people; but, although she was a good and gentle child who had not hitherto been ever disobedient to law and order, she never doubted now for a moment that she had done right. Her aunt Freda would at any other time have perceived on her return something unusual in her dreamy happy regard and her frequent reveries; but that great lady had lost her powers of observation or penetration, for she was absorbed in herself. She was discontented with herself; she was pusillanimous and insincere in her own eyes; she was angered against Syrlin for remaining in the country, and she was yet more angry with herself for being affected by it. It should have been as indifferent to her as the blowing of the rushes in the backwater by Willowsleigh.

She had gone down to Brakespeare the morning after her return to England, and in the sight of the health and strength of her children, and in the fine deep hues of the autumn landscape round the Castle, and the many claims on time and thought which her return brought with it, she endeavoured to forget this bitter sweetness, this sweet bitterness, which had come unawares into her life.

She had always liked the few quiet days which she got, now and then, before the advent of guests. She was alone for a week there; no one was expected for eight days to come; she walked and rode, alone or with her little boys under the reddened woods and the dusky angry skies. She was disturbed and troubled; she felt herself on the incline towards much that she had always disdained, always censured. For a woman to yield either to her senses or her sentiments had always seemed to her a miserable feebleness.

In this brief pause, when for a short space she was in comparative solitude at Brakespeare, she looked into her own heart and shrank from what she saw there. She was humiliated in her own sight, for she was conscious of entertaining opinions which were without courage, and emotions which were without legitimacy, and feelings which were in violent antagonism to all her views, and creeds, and laws of life. No one need ever feel what they do not wish to feel: so she had constantly said and believed. She had always considered that unwelcome sentiments only arose in those who weakly or willingly fostered them at birth. But as she rode or walked alone through the already bleak gardens and russet woods of the north, she became conscious of thoughts which invaded and regrets which assailed her, beyond any power of her own to dismiss them. And she despised herself with all the intensity of pride which was in her. An artist—a creature of caprice and vanity, and presumption and childishness!—a public favourite, whose talent had amused her, and whom she had used to pay her gold to see and hear as all the world did!—had power to haunt her memories, and make her untrue to all the traditions of her order and all the prejudices and principles of her life!

There were times when she hated her recollection of him, when if he had come before her she would have wished for the power of Mary to send him to the scaffold of Chastelard: and there were other moments when all that was warmer, truer, and more generous in her realised the beauty of his genius and the value of his homage, and was conscious of the want of courage and the want of generosity—even of common gratitude—in her treatment of him.

'Why will they come in our world?' she thought impatiently. 'We always hurt them and insult them. They are a people apart. They are children, fools—inspired lunatics, but always lunatics—they should not come amongst us, correct and slighting and artificial and conventional as we are: they please us at first and then shock and irritate us, and we have nothing in common with them; we do not see with the same eyes or hear with the same ears as they, and they offend us and we hurt them.'

All the exigencies of her life seemed to close in and weigh on her. The routine which to outsiders looked such variety, and the burden which to envious lookers-on seemed such freedom, the gall of position, the chains of custom, the fret of that continual publicity which no one who is a leader of society can escape, all these appeared a weariness to her flesh and to her soul. She tried to persuade herself that it was her vexation at the intention of her cousin to make so unsatisfactory a marriage, her irritation at the inertia and unwisdom by which her political party had been recently conspicuous; her offence at the unworthy suspicions and the circuitous dissembling which had marked her husband's conduct to herself and others; but as she was a woman who was not easily contented with affectations, she could not take refuge long in these attempts at self-delusion. She knew, and was bitterly angered with herself for the knowledge, that another and more personal feeling had 'sicklied over' the serene horizon of her thoughts.

But philosophy and analysis failed to content her, or drive out of her that abiding desire for the presence of another person which seemed to her so great and miserable a weakness. She had so long known all that was best, greatest, and most seductive in the world, and no adulation had moved, no seduction had fascinated her; she had gone on her way, calm, indifferent, kind, but callous, often moved to amusement and derision, never stirred to response; she had never for an instant believed in that overwhelming and irresistible magnetism which draws two human lives together against their will, and in opposition to all their interests. But some perception of its fatal force came to her as she passed her few days of liberty in the stately silences of Brakespeare, while the autumn mists rose from the mere over the river and the first frosts silvered the garden lawns.

The weather, for the north of England, was fine, though rather boisterous; she was glad to face those strong winds blowing from the North Sea one day, and the next from the heather lands of Scotland, although they made havoc amongst the gorgeous dahlias and chrysanthemums of the gardens and shook down the late tea-roses in fragrant showers over the grass.

In a week's time her husband arrived at the Castle, and the first circle of guests followed on the next day; and the routine which now seemed so intolerable to her began to unroll its length, a pale dull ribbon to her, though to many lookers-on it appeared as full of processions and colour as the tapestry of Beauvais.

'I am very much provoked that Syrlin would not come; they are always so thin-skinned and tenacious, these people,' Avillion said on the evening of his arrival; and he looked at her with a suggestive smile hovering upon his handsome mouth.

'You are difficult to content,' she answered with ill-concealed impatience. 'You forbade him your house a very little while ago. Why should you be so extremely anxious now to get him into it?'

'I told you,' said Avillion with bland civility, 'I wished to make him amends for my rudeness. And as people talk still of—of that very remarkable scene, it is desirable that he should be seen as my guest.'

She was silent.

'Suppose *you* asked him to come?' he murmured in his softest tone.

'I do not see the necessity,' she replied very coldly.

'No?' It was but a little insignificant monosyllable, and, softly spoken, scarcely stirred the silence, but it seemed to her to contain whole volumes of insult, of suggested condonation, of arranged complaisances, of odious suggestions.

'I have asked Mme. de Charolois. Be content,' she said, while an anger wholly new to her in its impetuosity flushed up in her regard and darkened her countenance.

'Mme. de Charolois! What has she to do with it?' repeated Avillion with the most innocent air of astonishment. 'Is *she* in love with your *beau ténébreux* then?'

She did not reply, but rose and went away. She was conscious that he was endeavouring to irritate and compromise her in her answers, and she was unequal to this kind of duel of duplicity. Other women found that sort of dissimulation easy, interesting, exciting, and useful; but she, frank by nature and proud to arrogance, could not descend to the indignity and cowardice of it.

Avillion offered her by suggestion, as plainly as though he had put in it words, that kind of pact, of tacit agreement, which is so common in the world but which had always seemed to her so poor, so pusillanimous, and so mean. She did not perceive the full drift of his intentions. She did not know that his ultimate desire and object was to draw her on to compromise herself beyond recall; she did not realise that his hidden but supreme desire was to be able ultimately to separate himself from her with the world's approval. She had no glimpse or suspicion of the final aim of his intentions, or the interior springs of his motives; but she saw that he was willing to encourage what he evidently believed to be her present weakness, and her whole temperament rose in offence and indignation at the tacit offer of permission and peace.

She did not realise that she had become more than indifferent to him, that she had become odious; and that he was therefore ready and willing to aid her to any act or sentiment which should place her in the wrong in the world's sight. She only saw very imperfectly into his views and motives, but what she did see was intolerable to her; the remembrance of his slow, sweet, suggestive smile was unendurable.

'After ten years that I have kept his name unblemished for him, can he know me so little as that?' she thought, with hot tears of pain rushing for a moment to her eyes. It wounded her in her self-esteem: it hurt her with a curious sense of his ingratitude, of his unworthiness, and with a woman's injustice and unreason she blamed Syrlin passionately. Why had he worn his heart on his sleeve, why had he stayed in England, why had he given cause for the world's comment and her husband's conclusions? It was the headstrong, selfish, inconsiderate feeling of a man who was outside society and had no stake to win or lose in it.

Everything seemed to her to have grown tangled and wrong, and her own influence on others to be either useless or wholly mischievous.

There had been a good deal of superb unconscious vanity in the enjoyment which she had possessed in her power over others, but this was gradually falling from her and leaving behind in its stead a depressing sense of incompetence and uselessness.

Syrlin refused the invitation to Brakespeare, Mme. de Charolois accepted it. The lord of Brakespeare was as usual favoured by a fortune beyond his merits. He had what he wished and paid no penalty for it.

Yet he was incensed against an artist who presumed to refuse the white flag of truce when he himself deigned to present it.

The absence of Syrlin disconcerted him in many ways; it upset his combinations and delayed his observations.

'Freda has told him to stay away, of course,' he thought when he received the curt note of refusal.

Syrlin did not take even the trouble to plead previous engagements. He was in his own house, and he remained in his own house, although the autumnal river fogs gathered around it.

'Passing even these horrible months in the Thames Valley!' said Avillion with a significant smile. 'If he spend the winter there too, the lady, whoever she be, who inspires such a melancholy passion will have to answer for the loss of his voice and the introduction of Ruy Blas to river rheumatics!'

It was said in his usual tone of half goodhumoured and half ill-natured banter, as a man speaks of trifles which do not concern him; but he gave a fleeting glance from under his lids at his wife, who supported it with that entire absence of all expression which is the mask of a woman of the world.

'It is our own fault,' he said petulantly to Claire de Charolois, to whom he had prematurely promised recitations by Syrlin. 'We have asked these people to our tables and made them our companions. They do not perceive that they are in reality no more than the jesters and the jongleurs of the middle ages, and they give themselves all the airs of fine gentlemen.'

'Are you so great an admirer of Syrlin that you regret him so?' asked Mme. de Charolois.

Avillion hesitated, then added with a little sigh :

'I know him very slightly. My wife and he are great friends. That scene in the Park was, I confess, very annoying to me; of course the young man behaved admirably, but the whole thing was a little theatrical and probably unnecessary, and any publicity of that sort is so disagreeable.'

'Why would she go out on such a day? I believe everyone knew it was dangerous,' said Mme. de Charolois.

'Oh, yes; but my lady is headstrong, though she looks so calm. Besides, *I* had especially written from Paris to beg her to stay at home, and that, of course, sufficed to send her out!'

'How very hard on you,' murmured the Duchess, who was beginning to find much sweetness in these revelations of his sorrows.

'Well, it pained me in this instance,' he said, with a resigned sad smile. 'But all the world thinks my wife an angel of gentleness and discretion, and believes she is sacrificed to me!'

'The world always sees such a very little way,' said Mme. de Charolois with sympathy, ' and its judgments are often at fault.'

Imperceptibly he had produced on her the impression that his wife made him extremely unhappy, and that he merited a better fate. Her interest in him troubled her conscience, for she was really devout and of a spiritual temperament; but she could not wholly resist his charm. There is no flattery so delicate and potent as the submission of those who have never been known to submit, and the whole attitude of Avillion towards her was indicative of homage and devotion. That mixture of sensuality and fancy which did duty in him, as in so many men, for the passion of love, had seldom been more strongly excited than it was excited by the young and saintly Frenchwoman, with her air as of a tall white lily set in a silver sacrament vase; and as he was master of all the forms of seduction, he knew precisely how to attract without alarming, and trouble without alienating, her, whilst every hour of the day he gave her to understand, without ever startling her by saying so, that he and all he possessed were wholly at her disposal.

It was to her that all the amusements and arrangements at Brakespeare were referred, and any trifling whim expressed by her was regarded as a law. His wife offered no opposition and made no comment.

'Lady Avillion never cares,' said the guests staying there. 'Freda never minds,' said her own people. Some blamed her and some praised her. Some thought it wise and some thought it foolish. Some said that it was nice of her and some said that it was odious in her. But no one perceived that beneath her serenity, her impassiveness, and her courtesy, she was for the first time in her life seriously unhappy. Mechanically she discharged all those onerous duties which devolve on the mistress of a great house. She never appeared to relax for a moment in her attention to others, and her solicitude for their comfort and amusement; she took her due share in the diversions which marked the various hours; and at evening she put on her great jewels, and her riband of Victoria and Albert, and sat in the centre of the table with an ever-ready smile and a never-failing politeness.

'She does it so well,' said her admirers. Yes, she did it very well; she had done it so long that it was second nature to her, but her husband, who was a very close observer, looking across at her saw that there was a line or two about her mouth and a droop in her eyelids which were new there, and which betokened her thoughts far away and her mind ill at ease.

'These virtuous women make themselves so needlessly miserable!' he said to himself; oddly enough including his wife and the Duchess de Charolois in the same reflection.

The situation interested him. He had not been interested for years. He had never wished for anything without almost immediately possessing himself of it ; a monotony of success as unexciting in its uniformity as a monotony of failure. Now for the first time in his life he was really in love with a woman who gave, and would give, him a great deal of trouble ; whilst his wife's development of character, although his intense irritation against her grew in hostility every hour, was a psychological study which his intelligence could penetrate and appreciate.

She had heard nothing of Syrlin except that brief refusal of the invitation to Brakespeare. She knew that he was passing the late autumn on the banks of the Thames, so ill-suited alike to his tastes and his health, but she knew no more. He had never replied by a word to the lines which she had written to him from London ; and such silence expressed more acutely to her than any reproach or rebuke could have done, how cold, how poor, how ungrateful, how ungracious her neglect of him must appear in his eyes.

'Ralph is right,' she thought. 'The lowest Jew or Moor or Arab in Morocco would have recompensed him better than we have done. We have not even the decency to show ourselves his friends.'

For she knew that the invitation of Avillion had been dictated by no sentiment which would bear examination, whilst her own solitary letter had been so poor of spirit, so trivial, and so commonplace, that she felt the temper and the spirit of Syrlin must condemn her with scorn and condemnation.

The very scum and filth of the streets had been moved to some sense of his courage and his daring; the very mob had cheered him; the wretched creatures who had recoiled from the hoofs of the Life Guards' chargers had had enough perception of what was fine, of what was gallant, of what was chivalrous, to applaud him, and leave him, unharmed, safe passage through their midst, and only they— she and her own people, her own world,— had been such conventional cowards that they had shrunk from openly declaring what she had owed to him!

'How he must despise us!' she thought a hundred times a day, as she went through the routine of her life at Brakespeare during these autumn weeks of ceremony and festivity.

Yet, why would he make himself so conspicuous? She was impatient and intolerant of his retreat from the world, his abjuration of all the pleasures of his age and habits. It was the kind of melodramatic withdrawal from the world which was most certain to attract the wonder and the curiosity of others. It might become the *Fernando* of the 'Favorita,' the *Didier* of 'Marion Delorme,' but in their period, in their society, in such a country as England, and such an epoch as this, it was absurd, incongruous, against all canons of good taste. Why could he not have gone to his city of Apuleius amongst his brethren the Nomads and his fathers the monks?

She knew that what she felt was ungrateful, unworthy, poor of spirit; but her dignity was dearer to her than any other earthly thing, and it seemed to her that her dignity was compromised when her world and her lord connected the hermitage in the Thames Valley with the scene in Hyde Park. Any advertisement of any feeling was in her view a concession to weakness, a permission to the daws of envy and slander to peck where they could wound, a hostage given, not only to fortune, but to enmity.

If the conventional laws of the world gall and harass, and fill with revolt and scorn those who are independent of them, such independence does not the less prick, bruise, and irritate those who from caste and custom deem those conventional laws necessary and excellent. Mary's heart might ache for Rizzio, but none the less did the stain of blood on the floor offend her royal eyes. Men may die for love, but they should find some pretext for their death.

The sense that the men and women of her world might be, nay almost certainly were, connecting in their suppositions and gossipries her own self with the abrupt change in the way of life of Syrlin, made a cruel and unkind feeling harden her heart towards him, and condemn his actions as theatrical and thoughtless. He should have thought of her, not of himself; he should have foreseen and understood the observations and deductions that such Jaques-like seclusion and melancholy would create. Almost she turned and shared the ingratitude and the injustice with which her people, and her husband's people, had rewarded his defence of herself. She despised their selfish and narrow coldness, and yet in a degree it bounded her own horizon, shrunk up her own emotions.

There is nothing so unkind and obdurate as the anger with which a conventional and vain temper sees itself compromised and lowered by the imprudence of another. And she was conventional to the core, although she was unaware of it; and she was vain, although her vanity was like her pride and her courage, of a splendid and lofty kind.

When her party at Brakespeare finally broke up, and her last circle of guests took their departure, she went on a series of visits to other great houses, spending two days here, four days there, twenty-four hours in this place, and the 'inside of a week' in that, in that routine of magnificent ennui which makes a mere toiler on a tread-mill, a mere blinded mule pacing the circular path of a turning-wheel, of fashionable life in England. The treadmill is gilded and covered with velvet, the mule is draped with jewelled housings, indeed, and fine tassels hang at its ears, but the monotony of the movement is scarcely lightened by its decoration.

She had never been so sensible of its tedium and of its incessant self-repetition as she was this autumn as she carried her gracious smiles and her ineffable indifference from one great house to another, north, south, east and west.

To several of the houses Avillion accompanied her, on the same principle which made him put up painted windows in churches; but he met the Duchess de Charolois at many of them, for his world wished to please him, and as she had recently visited at Brakespeare no one could see anything like connivance or contrivance in so slight an attention to the wishes of a popular and powerful gentleman.

'My wife can have her hermit-crab asked too, shell and all, if she likes,' Avillion said to himself, feeling that he was just and generous to magnanimity in his willingness to concede to her a full and free *quid pro quo*. Many men enjoyed the *quo* continually in all ways and never dreamed of giving their wives the slightest shadow of a *quid* in return. His supreme egotism had made him willing to accept any compromise which would favour and facilitate his own projects. Even that sensitiveness as to the honour of his name, which previously had survived all the corruption which self-indulgence and cynicism bring in their train, was now subservient to his willingness to see his wife compromise herself, since it would assist his own wishes. But, baffled and irritated by the slow drifting of events, he wondered fretfully was it possible that his wife was really as cold and passionless as he had always himself considered her to be?

'Lady Avillion looks unwell,' said Mme.

de Charolois to him one day; and he was very much irritated at the idea that she should do so. 'If she is going in for impregnable virtue and hopeless platonics it will make her infernally disagreeable and will be of no use to me,' he thought, with the petulant chagrin of a child who sees his playtime spoilt because another child will not understand how to throw its ball with precision and fly its toy-balloon with lightness, how to properly handle its playthings. Life was a game of give and take; as he was in the mood to concede the freedom which he enjoyed, it seemed to him odious perversity on the part of his wife not to accept what he so liberally offered. His feeling against her grew every day more harsh and more cruel; as his indifference had deepened to dislike, so his dislike sharpened into antipathy, and so more and more carefully did he cloak it in a politeness and an amiability which should lead her to believe him the trustful and generous dupe which he had feigned to her to be in his interview with her before her sojourn at Marienbad. All this scheming interested him keenly, and roused him from the apathetic satiety which had so often marred all his endeavours to be amused. But the perpetual absence of Syrlin perplexed and baffled him. 'Do they write to each other? Do they meet in secret?' he wondered. He endeavoured, with all the tact he possessed, which was much—for he had always found it a delicate instrument very useful to him—to have Syrlin present at some one of the houses where they visited. He praised him so gracefully, regretted his misanthropy so cordially, and referred to him so often as the only person who had ever made existence tolerable at Brakespeare, that there was a general effort made to induce the misanthrope to leave his solitude and bestow his presence on this or that or the other country-house filled for its late autumn meetings with the 'best people' of the great world. But none of these efforts succeeded; and to every invitation and entreaty written and telegraphed to him, Syrlin returned the same form of refusal: he required rest and was engaged in study.

Nothing moved him from this, and from the only person admitted to his hermitage, Auriol, nothing more than this could be elicited.

'Do you never see your idol now?' a woman inquired of Beaufront, who was giving a series of house-parties at Deloraine.

'Nobody sees him,' Beaufront replied with moroseness. 'He may be dead of damp and quinsy for aught I know. I can't imagine myself what charm he finds in a backwater.'

He was too absorbed in his own regret and desires, and too irritated against his cousin, to trouble himself to notice or to inquire what was the true meaning or the probable issue of Syrlin's long and remarkable withdrawal from the world. 'He is sulking,' he said, as Avillion said it, as Auriol said it; if Syrlin chose to make himself ridiculous he might do so; Beaufront was not disposed to meddle with him. Syrlin had the world before him, with every facility for enjoying it and every gift which could make him celebrated in it. If he chose to moon his months away aimlessly, in grey weather and studious solitude, let him: he might easily do more harm still, thought Beaufront grimly; remembering and not pardoning that gesture with which his friend had refused to take his hand. The perversity and ingratitude of all to whom he was himself attached seemed to Beaufront a very malice of the gods in his despite.

Consuelo Laurence had gone to the South of France with friends, and the shutters were shut in the pretty house in Wilton Street. He had sworn that he would not speak to her or write to her again, yet he had gone there as he had passed through London, and although he had known that she could not be in town that season, yet the sight of the closed shutters, the flowerless balconies, and the melancholy figure of the butler nursing the cat in his arms, in a hall shrouded in calico, had chilled his heart and embittered his humour.

'It's odd as the Duke don't know Madam's moves,' said the butler pensively to the cat. 'They've been as thick as thieves all these years, and now when I say she's away he just stares and stares as if he was turned to a pillar of salt, and then goes along the street with his head hung down. Hang me if I didn't always think that Madam would have managed to catch him at last! I think she might now, if she come back and looked sharp.'

The butler could no more conceive a state of things in which it would be possible for his mistress to refuse to become Duchess of Beaufront than he could have imagined the sparrows ringing the bells of St. Paul's. The views of upper servants are usually an exact replica of that of the best society, and motives of generosity or delicacy are as little taken into account by one or by the other.

Beaufront went down to Deloraine and discharged what was to him one of the dreariest duties of his position, wishing the while that the world had but one neck and he the delightful mission of cutting through it.

'What a stupid life, what a senseless life, what a wretched life!' he thought fiercely, as his illustrious visitors dined, waltzed, rode, drove, shot, hunted, and otherwise amused themselves on his domain, whilst he concealed his yawns as best he could, and smothered his oaths in his cigar; and when his social obligations had thus been discharged and he could once more feel his days free and his nights his own, he went to Heronsmere and spent the time in drawing pictures in his mind of Consuelo Laurence as she would look in those dim old galleries, in those dusky clipt yew walks, in those Haddon-like terraces where the peacocks perched on the stone balustrades and the soft west wind from the sea-coast stirred amongst the heavy interlaced boughs of the rosethorn. The place was made for her and she for the place. Why would this devil of pride, this insanity of self-sacrifice, keep her away from it and him?

One woman might have persuaded her, might still persuade her of the sincerity of his desires and the truth that his happiness was involved in the fulfilment of them; but that one woman was obstinately indifferent, perversely hostile, and would aid and countenance him in no way.

'No one is necessary to herself,' he thought bitterly ; 'how can she understand that others feel the need of sympathy, of companionship, of affection ? She is sufficient for herself ; she always will be to the end of time. It is of no use to speak to her of these things, she despises them. She cannot understand why one whom I know so intimately, whom I trust so entirely, in whom I feel repose and peace and comfort, is delightful to me after the racket of the world and the vileness of its subserviency and timeserving. All she sees is that, if I marry Consuelo, nine-tenths of my acquaintances will say I have married an adventuress who has been my mistress for years. Well, what does that matter ? Who cares ? Not I. I shall never love any other woman, and if I do not marry her I will live alone all my days, and let the dukedom die out—damnation to the dukedom !'

He was restless and unhappy as he paced up and down those long and tranquil terraces with which the graceful figure of Consuelo Laurence would have been so excellently in keeping. There was something amiss and ajar in his life now that he had neither her gentle and intelligent companionship nor even her letters, which had in absence always been so welcome to him. She was one of those women who wrote well, said neither too much nor too little, and conveyed to their correspondents a sense of sympathy which annihilated distance. But since that brief letter with which she had definitely rejected his repeated prayers, he had heard nothing of her, and pride, a man's stubborn, stiff-necked pride, forbade him to address her again. 'I swore that I would not,' he told himself again and again, and he kept his oath.

As he looked over the rolling woods and winding streams and wide green hills of Heronsmere, he laughed a little wearily and bitterly.

'For a man *à bonnes fortunes*, as they have always esteemed me, my fate is not brilliant. I have uselessly loved one woman who does not care even to perceive it, and I have offered to marry another who does not even believe in my wishing it,' he thought, with that sense of having given his treasure away to remain with empty hands, of having wasted a world of tenderness on a person to whom tenderness seemed but mere foolishness, which is the most painful form of all barren and futile regrets.

His cousin had been precious to him beyond all other living women, but of this she had known nothing, and to it, had she known, she would have been completely, supremely indifferent. The time had been, not long past either, when Beaufront would have gone down into battle to save the down of her fan from a speck of dust, or the splendour of her name from the faintest suggestion unworthy of it; but she had heaped ice on the warmth and candour of his emotions, and she had received the sensitive plant of his confidence with an unkind incredulity and derision. He was wounded and mortified; for more years than he cared to count her memory and her presence had disturbed his peace and robbed all other women of charm for him. Her slight, cool smile seen across the crowd of a Throne-room or a Drawing-room had long banished all warmth and interest from his existence, and still when he heard the sweet homely song of the mavis or blackbird in his own summer woods, the mornings of her childhood in the green glades of Bellingham came over his remembrance with that pang of regret which never wholly passes : the regret for what might have been, for the day which can never be recalled, for the flower which no forces in nature can ever call again into bloom. Those moments recur but rarely in the life of a man of the world, but during their brief duration they overcast all the fair weather of fortune, and the dejection which they leave behind them grows sometimes into a chronic malady of temper and of mind. Beaufront, courted by everyone and envied by most, had the same sense of isolation which weighed on the youth Flodden. There was no heart which grew gayer or sadder merely because he smiled or sighed. He could have found hundreds who would have simulated such sympathy, but he could have found none who could have satisfied him as to their sincerity.

As the year wore to its close he met his cousin in two or three houses where habit and party and friendship all combined to necessitate his attendance sorely against his will. By tacit agreement they saw and said as little of and to each other as appearances permitted. He thought, as Mme. de Charolois thought, that she looked unwell.

There was a worn look upon her proud fair features which was altogether new there, and an irritability which she did her best to control often ruffled that serene and at times cruel composure, and the suave semblance of courteous interest in all around her, which had been her distinguishing characteristics.

'She is not happy,' thought Beaufront with regret; 'perhaps she would feel for what I feel? Could one only make her understand!'

They were at that moment staying, at the same time, at Lord Greatorex's, on one of those state-visits to a Chief of Party which are as obligatory as visits to a sovereign. There had been a marriage, and a coming of age, in the Greatorex family, which was a very domestic one, and the double event had given rise to those hospitalities which are as terrible to the givers as to the receivers. Patrician England had been entertained almost *en masse*, and patrician England had smiled on its face and yawned in its sleeve.

Avillion alone had not yawned, because Mme. de Charolois was there, looking like a picture of Lionardo's, with her cloud of dusky hair shadowing her pale and pensive face.

'So exquisite,' he said to himself; 'a

woman who only looks lovely and says next to nothing, who is at once one's delight and despair.'

'He has never admired anyone for so many consecutive weeks,' said his wife, with that intonation of disdain which was as soft as the south wind and as cold as the north. 'Mme. de Maintenon was a wise creature; she has recorded the potent charm of the *jamais content et jamais désespéré.*'

She was standing by a lake in Lord Greatorex's stately home park, and in the gardens afar off, but within sight, Avillion and the French Duchess were strolling; he shivering though wrapped to the eyes in Russian sables, and she willingly courting the sharp autumn wind which she knew might blow as it would on her lily-like skin without reddening its satin-soft whiteness.

Beaufront, who found himself near her by the pretty waters of the bird-haunted mere, looked over his shoulder at the distant figures and muttered an angry word.

'You are too good to him,' he said curtly.

'He wants a lesson.'

'A lesson to a grown man means a scene. Surely you would not counsel that? Besides, what does it matter?'

'It has always mattered to those who care for you.'

'Oh no, it is no one's business, and, I repeat, it does not matter. Besides, a woman in society does not compromise him so much as some other things have done in their time.'

'You are too patient.'

'Indifference is always patient.'

Beaufront was silent.

It always hurt him to hear her speak of her husband.

They were alone for the moment; others were near, but she had gone a little apart where the larches and hollies grew close beside the water in a little hollow where the east wind did not come, and Beaufront had joined her there, drawn out of his sullen avoidance of her by that magnetism which she had always exercised so strongly and so unconsciously over him. She had seated herself for an instant on a root-chair which had been made there between two silver larches; the symmetry and grace of her figure were shown to perfection as the pallid sunshine shone through the leafless boughs; the dark cloak she wore enhanced the brilliancy of her complexion and her hair. He stood near, now and then picking a pebble off the ground

and sending it in a long straight flight across
the little lake.

'You are not happy,' he said impulsively,
knowing that he spoke unwisely, using that
language of sentiment which she despised.

'Oh, yes,' she replied, 'I am as happy as
women ever are; I do as I like in most things,
and I have grown as used to the kind of life
I lead, as carriage horses get used to prancing
down the drive. I suppose the horse by
nature was not meant to be a dressed-up
creature with a bit in its mouth, but if it
was made for anything else, it has forgotten
what that anything else could possibly have
been like.'

'Habit is not happiness,' said Beaufront.

'It is the apology for it with which most
people have to be content.'

'There is a kind of happiness which does
not pass. It comes from sympathy.'

Freda Avillion laughed drearily.

'Oh, I know those great affinities; they
usually end in a furious quarrel because the
man is seen with another woman at Ascot, or
because the woman has danced too often with
another man at the New Club. You have had
many of those sympathies in your time, my
dear Ralph.'

'That is not what I mean,' said Beaufront with annoyance. 'If you do not know what I do mean, perhaps you will some day.'

'The fair encounter of two most rare affections?' said his cousin. 'Of course I know what you mean by that, and what Shakespeare meant. You mean what we all think of when we are young; some glory which shall never end or change or rust. But what do we see in reality? What is love as it is found in the world? Only a liaison which is very delightful for a season or two and then is outgrown and cast off; or a marriage which begins with idolatry and drifts into indifference. For six months they cannot live without each other; the year after they are bored if they have to dance in the same quadrille at a ball; he thinks what a hideous colour she washes her hair, and she thinks that he is actually getting fat! It is always like that. One sees it five hundred times every season.'

'There is too much like that, certainly.'

'Did you ever care for one person yourself for any length of time?'

Beaufront hesitated.

'Not for any woman who ever was mine,' he replied.

She was far from dreaming that there

was any personal allusion to herself in the reply.

'What a true man's answer,' she said with amusement. 'And many women are like that also in our world. And yet you, as if you were a poet, think love is necessary to happiness.'

'Do you remember what I asked of you at Marienbad?' he said abruptly.

'Oh yes,' she replied carelessly. 'Do you still retain the same fancy?'

Beaufront laughed joylessly.

'At my age one does not change that sort of "fancy" every month. What I said to you was said on deliberate consideration. There is but one person who could give me the kind of companionship which I wish for ; and you are hostile to her ; you more than any other have so acted as to imbue her with the impression that her marriage with me would make me absurd in the eyes of my world.'

'Absurd, no. It would lower you certainly,' she said coldly.

'It seems to me wholly useless to go over all the ground again.'

'It is not my opinion only ; it is that of all our own people. It would be your own if you were passing judgment upon any other person.'

'It is certainly very easy to be wise for others,' said Beaufront. 'Wise or unwise, I know what I wish, and in your perpetual hostility to a woman to whom I am deeply attached you have done me an injury which is none the less real because you do not choose to believe in it.'

'An attachment of habit? That is what so often makes a liaison end in a marriage; but I never heard the friends of the man who made such a marriage consider it a good one for him.'

The brows of Beaufront contracted angrily, and his eyes darkened with a sombre wrath.

'I have told you that I have had no liaison with Mrs. Laurence, and I expect to be believed.'

'In anything else I believe you,' said Lady Avillion not unkindly, but with a bland obstinacy which infuriated him. The anger of a man against a woman is increased and embittered by its entire impotence to let itself loose even in words upon her. She is a woman, she is a gentlewoman; he cannot even tell her in passionate language of the indignation with which every drop of blood in his body is thrilling.

His cousin looked at him without sympathy; she considered that he was telling her an untruth, as a man tells one in a witness-box when questioned as to his relations with a woman. She did not blame him, but the continuance of the comedy wearied her.

'I do not know why you should select me as your confidante,' she said, in a tone which testified how little interest the subject was to her. 'You might as well tell your sisters and ask their intervention. They have been quite as much prejudiced against your friend as I have been.'

'My sisters and everyone else followed your lead,' said Beaufront, with a deep anger vibrating in his sonorous voice. 'You have done a mischief which you probably could not undo, even if you ever wished to undo it. You ask why I confide in you; God knows I am a fool to do so, for I could not find any confidante less sympathetic in the whole human race. But I will tell you why I have been moved to do so; you are the only woman whom I have ever loved.'

'My dear Ralph! What folly!'

'Not folly in any way, and entirely the truth. You are not to blame for it. You have coquetry enough in your own grand fashion with others, but with me you have had none. Yet I have loved you ever since you were a child at dear old Bellingham when I taught you how to sit your pony and how to thrash the water with your rod. Of course I said nothing to you; I was a beggar, with no chance of property or position; and you, you married Avillion. Perhaps you never could or would in any case have married me; I do not at all suppose you would, you were too used to me; but that memory, that possibility, that "might have been," has chilled and jarred my life for me. I gave you all the best I had to give. You withered up my heart for me *sans le savoir, sans le vouloir.* I know that you do not believe in these things, but you may do so. And this is the reason why you should have patience for, and pity on the affection which I feel for Consuelo Laurence. It is not passion certainly, it is not such love as I could have felt for you; but it is an extreme tenderness, a great need of her, a profound sense that she would be to me what her name implies— Consolation. I do not know why I say this to you, except that there are times when one tires of keeping one's heart wrapped up in one's sleeve, and would sooner daws pecked at it than have it unnoticed. No doubt what I have said seems to you merely ridiculous, but it is the truth, and you may give it such pity as an honest truth deserves.'

He turned his head from her as he spoke. He was to the core a man of the world imbued with the cynical stoicism of such men, and it cost him much, was strange to him, and painful, to be touched to so much confession of emotion.

She was silent from utter astonishment; words which Syrlin had spoken to her at Heronsmere passing through her remembrance as she listened with no expression except a blank surprise upon her features. She did not know what to reply to him, she did not know whether she was touched or offended; but through her thoughts ran a faint egotistic taint of irritated vanity. He had loved her all these years, and he could find solace in Consuelo Laurence!

Beaufront stood still with his face averted from her. He was absently throwing stones across the water, watching them skim the surface and plunge out of sight in eddying circles.

'I don't know why I said this to you,' he said with a sigh, as he picked up another pebble. 'But if you take it as I mean it, it may make you kinder to her—to me.'

She looked across the mere with her dark blue eyes cold and irresponsive. What children men were to her, how poor and trivial and mutable!

'I scarcely follow the sequence of your reasonings,' she said in her chilliest, clearest, sweetest tones. 'You seem to say that I have long made you miserable, and that another lady can now make you happy. I cannot in the least see why that fact should draw her and me any nearer, and it only shows that men's ideals are Protean toys.'

Beaufront threw a pebble with so much violence and velocity that he startled from their resting-place a flock of wild duck, and sent them fluttering in alarm over the sedges and water-weed.

'You mean that you utterly refuse my request?' he said in a low tone.

'I do distinctly. If I have been Mrs. Laurence's predecessor in your sentiments, I am not inclined to be her sponsor in society,' she said with that little smile which always meant that her decision was immutable. 'You can marry her; I can clearly foresee that you will marry her; but you must get someone else to present the seventh Duchess of Beaufront.'

Beaufront turned from the rushy bank, the shining water, the screaming ducks.

'For twelve years,' he said harshly, 'I have thought you utterly thrown away on a heartless roué like Uther Avillion, but I now see that I was mistaken; your marriage is an admirably assorted one; it is *à cœur sec, cœur sec et demi.*'

'I am fortunate if it be so,' she said calmly, and she turned away from him, and being joined immediately by three or four gentlemen, passed with her graceful bearing and her perfect movement over the grass-lands towards the house.

CHAPTER XLVI

'It is the dreadful state of the country. They say we can't leave,' said Avillion plaintively, condoling, or affecting condolence, with himself for his presence, in wintry winds and icy rains, in his own land.

The state of the country was bad, as the state of it has been bad for the last ten years; as the state of every European country is in the old age of the present century; but its state, even had it been infinitely more desperate, would not have kept him in it a day had not Mme. de Charolois been pleased to go from one country-house to another showing her delicate beauty and her admirable skill in skating on the meres and ponds of stately English parks.

For her he even projected and endured a Christmas gathering at Brakespeare, where masques and carols and Twelfth Night dances were organised in the most brilliant and historically accurate manner, because such old-world pastimes amused her, and were said by her to suit, as they undoubtedly did, the majesty and ancientness of his castle.

In all these festivities, very splendid and protracted, his wife passively carried out what he desired, neither opposing nor originating ; the burden of these long series of entertainments fell upon herself, as it always must fall on the mistress of the house; but she supported it without apparent effort. It was all done for Claire de Charolois and she knew it, but she gave no sign that she did know it. Never before, since the accession of its present lord, had Brakespeare been an open house in mid-winter, when the snow lay deep on the moors around, and the frost kept the horses neighing and stamping in their stalls. Avillion looked out of the windows with a shudder, although the electric light and the best system of hot-air flues made the interior by day and by night warm and bright as Madeira or Madagascar.

'It is summer indoors, and it is the contrast which makes the charm,' said the Duchess in reproof. 'I wonder that you, who have so studied the philosophy of enjoyment, have not discovered the beauty of contrasts before.'

'You have taught me that beauty in your

own person,' he murmured tenderly. 'So fair, and yet so cold!'

She smiled: her pensive vacuous smile which so perplexed him. She was not clever, nor even intelligent, but she had a great power over him, born of the charm of mystery and of resistance ; such resistance as seems always on the brink of entire concession yet never wholly yields,

'I am really in love!' he said to himself a thousand times in amazement at his own durability of desire. And his bitterness against his wife increased with every hour, as every hour served further to increase his conviction that Claire de Charolois was the only woman who had ever lived who would have made him faithful to her.

He would not have been faithful to her had he been able to marry her. He would have found her tedious, taciturn, tiresome, and have quarrelled with her in a week's time. But nothing would now have convinced him of this, and he was as profoundly in love with her as it is possible for a supreme egotist ever to be with anyone. 'If I were only free!' he thought with the restless sullen rage of a child kept in school when he might be playing out in the garden.

He disliked waiting for anything, and he was tired of waiting to see the development of that to him extremely uninteresting character which everyone admired in his wife except himself.

'Virtuous women always take their *grandes passions* so desperately hard,' he said fretfully to himself; ' if I am goodnatured enough not to mind her amusements, why should she distress herself so unnecessarily ? ' It seemed to him that the obstinacy of women was wholly unendurable. 'Whatever you wish,' he mused, ' they oppose. When I was furious at her adoring the fellow, she was bent on making much of him ; and now that I do not object to what she does, she takes no notice of his existence. It is all perversity.'

He seriously and even passionately wished his wife to compromise herself. Enmity, malice, and many unholy feelings, all combined to make his present mood of hatred of her stronger than his love of his own good name. To have triumphed in her concession to human infirmities would have been so delightful to him that he would have purchased the enjoyment by acceptance of what he, like all other men, had always regarded as the most mortifying form of affront to honour.

He was so infinitely tired of seeing her at her place in his house, and of having to accompany her to courts and ceremonies, that he would have welcomed her greatest offences provided they had ridden him of her presence.

'She has always bored me,' he said plaintively to his sister, Lady Shropshire, really persuading himself that she always had.

She might be a lovely woman, a witty woman, an attractive woman to others; but to him she had always been absolutely without charm.

'But you always used to say that she suited you so excellently?' Lady Shropshire ventured to suggest to him deferentially, for his family always deferred to him.

'One must say something civil of one's wife,' said Avillion with a sigh. 'And if I did say it, which I do not think I ever did, I suppose it was to please Lady Greatorex.'

It certainly did not please Lady Greatorex that he, one of the columns of the Carlton, should only live in the light of a French Duchess's eyes; but Avillion had done a great deal for his party and could not wholly be sacrificed to that fetish.

The Greatorexes were eminently domestic

and virtuous people ; they had a large
progeny and lived amidst it like patriarchs of
old. Avillion was very terrible to them in
many ways ; but then he put up the painted
windows, invited the bishop of his diocese to
his Easter parties, and occasionally attended
Sunday service at the Chapel Royal. The
Greatorexes did not quarrel with a great Tory
gentleman so long as he did these things ; they
shut their eyes to everything except the number of figures in his political subscriptions,
and the weight of his Conservative influence in his county. If political leaders did
not know how occasionally to hunt with the
hounds and run with the hare, great political
organisations would soon fall to pieces.

Why had he ever married Wilfreda
Damer, who had never had any gratitude, any
sympathy, any comprehension of his character ? He asked himself this pettishly, in these
Christmas and New Year weeks.

She looked very well, certainly, and she
received very well, but that was all. 'You
want something more in your wife than a
femme qui dirige bien,' he said to himself, until
he really believed that his happiness had been
entirely blighted by her.

There is no sentiment which increases so

rapidly as a dislike which is felt for a person who is near in relation and frequently near in vicinity. No animosity is so intolerant, so unkind, so irreconcilable as that which arises from a once close intercourse, and which is embittered by the sense that it replaces what was once a passion. The sweetest wine makes the sharpest vinegar. Physical beauty or personal excellence can in no way diminish such an enmity; on the contrary, every familiar tone, every well-known gesture or expression, every turn of the head or movement of the hand increases it, and in all which once fed and nourished admiration, food is found to justify and increase a dislike which becomes as vigilant and as sensitive as once sympathy and appreciation were.

It was with such a hostile sentiment as this that he now regarded his wife, until everything which was admirable in her seemed to him odious; her dignity seemed stiffness, her patience seemed scorn, her calmness seemed irony, her obedience to his whims seemed servility and mere designing paltriness of spirit, and even her grace of movement as she passed him in a room appeared an absurd affectation which set all his nerves on edge.

He had never in his life attempted to

govern or eradicate any feeling that he felt, and he allowed free run to this irritated acrimony which grew up in him towards the mother of his children.

'Why is she the mother of my children?' he thought angrily; it really seemed to him her worst offence of all.

It was childish, but he was a spoilt child; it was unjust, but egotists are never just; it was illogical, but passions are not weighed or weighted by logic; and whenever he did not get exactly and instantly what he wanted he always considered that the whole world was in league and conspiracy against him.

'He thinks it so unkind that I do not die!' thought Freda herself, with that comprehension of his feelings towards her which had become so clear and so cold since that brief period of deception in which she had been his dupe.

During these brilliant winter festivities, to which all that was highest and gayest in English society was bidden, her sense of the inadequacy and artificiality of the life she led grew daily upon her. She had compared herself to the carriage horse which goes its daily round, caparisoned, with regulated pace and all nature in it repressed and obliterated. Nature awakened in her at times underneath the ever-smiling, ever-gracious composure with which she played the part so long familiar to her. The life of the world may in great measure become a substitute for a repression of the natural emotions and passions, but never wholly so as long as there is youth, so long as there is feeling; always at intervals will the latter stir and crave some indulgence, some portion, some hearing. The world is as a Nirvana, claiming, absorbing, pervading the existence of its believers; but at times it fails to satisfy what it permeates, at times its paradise seems poor and pulseless.

It so seemed to her in these winter weeks, when to please and flatter another woman all the resources of invention and wealth were exhausted in those great festivities at Brakespeare which were nominally given for the sake of stimulating and keeping together the wavering Tory feeling in the North. Lord Greatorex, taking thither his massive and Solon-like countenance, complimented and thanked the master of Brakespeare for his public spirit and self-sacrifice: and Avillion, with that admirable capacity for high comedy which characterised him, murmured softly: 'Oh, my dear friend! anything I can do—anything we can any of us do—you command me in every way. But, alas! who can command the weather?'

But all this high elaborate comedy, as much and as truly a comedy as the 'Misanthrope' or the 'Rivals,' became like a grotesque farce to Avillion's wife, although she took her part in it, and never failed to play that part to perfection.

Patriotism!—we yield everything inch by inch to clamour and to panic. Loyalty!—we receive princes, and make game of them as soon as they are gone. Ambition!—what is there that we want?—nothing that anyone can give us. Duty!—who knows what way it lies, what face it wears, what tongue it speaks? What can the oracles say to us, since we have all seen the augur hiding behind the altar, and know that the sacred voice is but the formula of the hidden priest?

So she thought, bitterly, this winter as she went through all the phases of the time, drove Lady Greatorex to the Habitation in the little red-roofed, brown-walled, northern town, went with her ladies to see the torch-lit sports on the frozen lake, received illustrious persons at the foot of the grand staircase, and led the quadrille *d'honneur* in the beautiful white ball-room of Brakespeare,

Sometimes a desire which she had never known before seized on her to get away from it all, to have it broken up and ended, to throw it off as she threw off her furs when she came in from the skating. Yet she could imagine no other life. This one was her native air. Its manners, its habits, its ways, its thoughts, its rules, were bred in her bone and grafted on her brain. She tried to think of herself as she would be if she left it all; living in obscurity in some foreign country place on the narrow income which her own slender dower would give her, living on rich thoughts and poor fare as Lorraine Iona counselled, living for the spirit, unconventionally, intellectually, apart from everything which she had known; she tried to realise such a fate for herself—but she could not prevail on her mind to draw any such picture in serious clear outlines.

Such women there might be; such women, no doubt, there had been; if Beaufront were to be believed such a woman at one period of her career had been Consuelo Laurence. But she herself could never become such a woman. The world was her element as was the water to Undine. She could not imagine any state in which she could live without it.

It had lost all seduction for her, all its disguises were stripped off it; it was a poor, aimless, joyless, hollow thing; but it was hers, she was its child, begotten by it and bound to it. She could not portray to herself any life without it.

She might have done so once, perhaps; but not now, never now.

And yet she was tired of it; she was intolerant of it: now and again she made certain slighting remarks of which the bitterness and scorn forced her hearers to open their eyes wide at such strange heresies coming from her lips.

'Lady Avillion is hipped,' said Lord Greatorex to his wife. 'Is there anything she could possibly like to have, do you know? Is it possible that we have neglected some wish or some request expressed by her?'

But it was not within the power of Lord Greatorex, great man and minister although he was, to give Freda Avillion what she wished or wanted. For she wanted freedom, and yet freedom would have been unendurable to her. She wanted love, and yet love would have been detestable to her. She wanted simplicity, and yet simplicity would have been odious to her. She wanted solitude, and yet solitude would have been to her still more insupportable than was the crowd in which she perpetually moved and had her being. When there is no gift which, being given, could be enjoyed by the receiver, both heaven and earth are powerless donors.

CHAPTER XLVII

IN the northern counties the frost was severe that winter, and the broad rapid river, by name the Swiftsure, which fed the forests of Brakespeare, was still bound under it, and the lake which closed in the gardens was a sheet of ice. The keepers broke holes for the fish to breathe and the swans and the wild fowl to drink at, and in the park the herds of deer came tamely to be fed, looking like beautiful statues of bronze against the silvered ferns and the whitened grass.

Claire de Charolois was an elegant and admirable skater, and knew that her tall frail lily-like form never looked more effective than when, arrayed in some close-fitting sealskin or sable, she seemed to float over the ice with the rapidity of lightning and the graceful curved flight of a crane. It carried out her views of the charm of contrast, for nothing could be in stronger contrast than the incredible swiftness and ease of her movements with the entire silence in which she moved, and the dreamy pensive absorbed gaze of her eyes, which seemed to look far away and see nothing of those around her.

It was to please her that her host organised the water-carnival upon the frozen lake and river, and himself appeared upon the ice shivering internally under his costly furs, but watching her with adoring eyes, lest she should feel fatigued, and hovering ever within her reach with a richly decorated eighteenth-century sledge, modelled by Gouthière, with panels painted by Fragonard and varnished by Martin.

Avillion, who could skate well, as he could do most things, but hated the exertion and dreaded over-heating himself, looked very handsome as he leaned on the back of this sledge waiting on the pleasure of the momentary idol of his fancy.

One day, fatigued at last, or feigning fatigue, Claire de Charolois approached the sledge, poised on her roller blades as lightly as an ibis on her wings.

'I am tired, you may drive me,' she said to Avillion as she stepped with her languid grace into the sledge-chair, whilst he, with the deference and reverence of a courtier of

Versailles, covered her knees with the ermine-lined rugs.

His wife standing at a little distance on the bank smiled slightly as she saw his attitude and guessed his words. Just so had he addressed herself a dozen years before when he had seen her with her roses in her hand standing on the lawn of Bellingham.

'*Tout lasse, tout casse, tout passe,*' she thought. 'But I could never have made him heat himself by pushing a chair for me over ice.'

For he who dreaded heats, who dreaded chills, who abhorred effort, and deemed all open-air exertion of the muscles ploughmen's work, was leaning on the back of the gilded and painted sledge, and moving it along the surface of the lake, whilst Mme. de Charolois bent her face over a bouquet of hothouse flowers with which he had presented her.

It was not with jealousy, nor even any sense of wrong or of offence, yet it was with a certain impulse of irritation that Freda stood watching them thus harmoniously glide along the shining snow-powdered expanse. There had been a tone in the few syllables spoken by the Duchess which carried with it the impression of a perfect understanding, of a complete familiarity, with the host whom she had thus commanded to be her valet. Used as his wife was to his inconstancies, something in that tone, in its serene authority, its matter of course permission to serve, moved her to impatience.

'Within my hearing! Under my eyes!' she said to herself. She was not astonished, she was not even affronted, but still it jarred upon her. Had it been anywhere else she would not have heeded it; but here, at Brakespeare, she felt herself insulted, and she despised herself as his accomplice.

May and Fluff, flushed and excited, dashed past her at that moment, their cheeks glowing, their eyes flashing, their hair flying, forgetful in the triumph of successful skating of their dignity and of the opinions of Lord Dover.

'Come!' shouted May, turning back his head to his mother, and she obeyed the appeal and went down the lake beside their children.

All out-of-door pastimes had been made easy and familiar to her in early days at Bellingham, and her skating was equal to Mme. de Charolois'. In the mood she was in at that moment the rapid rushing motion was welcome to her; the keen, fierce northern air was a tonic and a sedative in one. With her body perfectly balanced, and her arms folded, she glided on, the picturesque groups on the ice, the fringing alders and larches of the banks, the snow-covered rushes, the painted sledge-chairs, all passing by her with the swiftness of a swallow's flight. She soon distanced her little sons, her guests and friends, the gentlemen flying in her path. She put all the strength and energy which were in her, and which were great, into the contest. She was glad of the sharp air which stung her like a whip, and the swift movement which heated her veins and stilled her thoughts.

The lake was fed by a branch of the river, and this minor stream, now frozen like the river itself, was a deep narrow channel overhung with trees of various kinds. She knew where the outlet was, and went towards it, whilst the majority of the party remained on the garden side of the lake where the wind was less keenly felt, whither the children had turned also, attracted by the chair-sledging, and the buffet of tea, iced wines, and sweet and savoury dainties, which was placed under a tent on the bank, near a large Lebanon cedar.

'A caviare biscuit and a sugared almond are dearer to them than I,' thought their mother with a little laugh, as she sped onward towards the northern bank and turned into the narrow in-passage made by the little stream under the frosted boughs. Looking back she saw her sons already by the tent, their skates off and their hands filled with bonbons, which they were munching as squirrels munch nuts.

'If I died to-morrow,' she thought, 'they would only be very pleased with the "funeral baked meats" and the crape on their hats!'

But she felt very far from death as the blood tingled in her limbs with the rarefied air, and the glittering icicles on the boughs were dashed in her face as she glided on following the curves of the stream.

'Oh, leave me alone, I am so glad for once to be alone!' she said with involuntary warmth as one of the gentlemen at last reached her side. He was an old friend of her childhood, Lord Glastonbury, one of the many men who had loved her vainly. He was struck by the tone in which she spoke, hesitated a moment, looking wistfully at her, then obeyed her, and wheeled round to return to the lake.

'Take care, that is all; the ice further on is untried,' he said as he regretfully left her. He imagined that she was annoyed and disturbed, and wished for a few minutes' respite from the incessant demands on her of her many guests.

'Poor Glassy!' she thought as she sped away from him. 'He was always such a good creature, and never affronted whatever one said to him.'

The way to the great river was long, but it seemed short to her as the leafless trees flew by her, and the sharp strong wind blew in her face and pierced through the furs she wore. The landscape was austere and chill, the silence was unbroken; all sound and movement had been left behind with the pastimes on the lake; the afternoon sun grew low and very pale. The frozen channel which she followed wound in and out with many a turn always under the shadow of larch and alder, willow and hazel. It was a deep green stream famed for its trout in April weather, and banked by mossy earth thick sown with violet and primrose roots. It was one of the beauties of the home park, and a favourite drinking haunt of the deer. It was now frozen hard and firm as steel, and the low grey sky seemed almost to stoop and touch the trees.

No one would miss her, she thought, for half-an-hour, and the freedom, the solitude, were welcome to her. They were all laughing, skating, flirting, eating nougat, and drinking pineapple punch ; they would not notice her brief absence.

'I am always on guard,' she thought ; ' they may let me off duty for twenty minutes, I think.'

On skates one goes far in twenty minutes ; she wished to reach the Swiftsure itself, and see its grey, sombre winter beauty where it was wont to roll so boisterously, peat-stained, through its lofty hills and moors, and now they said was as motionless as its tributaries, chained down under the iron grip of the frost.

She went on and on, on and on ; she knew the course of the stream well, and knew how and when it would fall into the breast of its parent waters in reedy lonely places, which the bittern still haunted and the coot and the moorhen cherished. At last she reached that spot just as the dim sun sank out of sight behind the brown ridge of moorland covered with heather burnt black with frost. Heavy clouds, snow laden, floated slowly across the slope of the hills; on either side the forests stretched sombre and gruesome; in the foreground were beds of rushes and of reeds, frozen fast amidst sheets of ice, and beyond these was the larger river, level and white and smooth, with flocks of wild birds flying with shrill cries above its frozen surface. It was as lonely, as soundless, as melancholy, as though it had been in the fastnesses of unexplored hills on the shores of untraversed seas. The sun, sunk now wholly out of sight, left a faint eerie light upon the ice-bound waters and the blackened moors charred by frost as though by fire. She wound her way through islets of reeds and rushes towards the Swiftsure itself; she desired to see the view up and down its course, which at all seasons of the year was famous for its beauty. The ice cracked and bent between the osier-beds as she passed over it, but she passed on unheeding that warning sign; she was at all times courageous to folly. In another moment she would have been out and on the river itself, which here between the heather hills grew broad and lake-like, but a voice from the dusky shadows of the birch groves called aloud to her:

'For God's sake, stop! The ice of the

greater water will not bear; it will break beneath you.'

Instinctively she paused, and her face grew as white as the ice which sustained her; but the emotion which she felt was not fear: it was amazement, wonder, pleasure, pain, a thousand troubled emotions fused in one, for she recognised the voice which addressed her.

'Was it an hallucination?' she thought feebly and feverishly, for she saw no one; and she stooped and loosened her skates, and leaned against the stem of a birch-tree, for she was out of breath and disturbed by the strange tricks which her fancy played her.

Why should she hear that voice amidst these lonely hills and waters, unless her brain were foolishly filled with the memory of it?

She was angered against herself and ashamed of her own weakness. Some one of course, she reasoned, must have spoken, but it could only be some passer-by, some peasant or some pedlar, some one who did not know her by sight. That her fancy should have heard in it the accents of Syrlin made her ashamed of the persistency with which in solitude her thoughts reverted to him. But scarce a moment more elapsed before she realised that she had not been the dupe of the imagination; coming over the ice and through the yellow crackling reeds, she saw the figure of a man, rudely clothed as a moorland wanderer might be, with a knapsack on his back, and high boots reaching to the knee. As he approached her he uncovered his head, and the sharp wind blew in his dark curls, and the face, beneath that dusky glory of blowing hair, was the face of Syrlin.

She was so amazed and stupefied that she spoke not a word, but stood gazing blankly at him, still doubting the testimony of her own senses.

'Forgive me,' he murmured, whilst the blood leapt to his cheeks and the flame to his eyes. 'I should not have dared to speak, but in another moment you would have been out on the river ice and it would have broken beneath you.'

The grey and silvery atmosphere around them, the pale weird light, the dark and leafless woods, the frozen waters, made a scene with which the virile yet poetic beauty of the man before her was in perfect harmony. He had been so constantly in her thoughts since her return to England that his sudden presence was a shock to her rather painful than pleasurable, yet stirring all her nature to its depths.

For the first time in her life she was speechless from strong emotions which she did not analyse, and which for the moment had greater force than herself.

'It is like a scene on the stage,' she thought with anger, a moment later. 'Will he never remember that I am not Doña Sol nor Célimène?'

He saw the anger in her blue dark eyes, and he did not resent it; she would not have been what she was had she welcomed him like tenderer or weaker women.

'What are you doing here?' she said very coldly when she recovered her voice. 'You refused Lord Avillion's invitations persistently; it is not usual to approach a house after such refusals, though I am quite sure that he will be charmed to welcome you.'

Syrlin coloured hotly.

'I shall not trouble Lord Avillion's hospitality. I should not even have spoken to you had you not been in danger of your life.'

'Are you always to play the part of my Providence?' she said coldly. 'Allow me to say that I do not care for such unexpected appearances, even when they are useful: they are too dramatic.'

She was sensible of the injustice and the ingratitude of the words, but she spoke them almost despite herself. If anyone saw her here, or heard of such a meeting, what could it ever appear except a rendezvous?— a rendezvous of the most sensational and the most vulgar kind! The romance, the impetuosity, the acknowledged ardour shown by his appearance there, jarred on all the habits of her ways and thoughts: such things were beautiful in verse, or romantic prose, but not in real life within three miles of Brakespeare and of Lady Greatorex!

Syrlin, standing beside her under the alder and larch boughs, was gazing at her with his fervent lustrous eyes, and was so absorbed in his contemplation that he was barely conscious of the cold words which so cruelly received him.

'What are you doing here?' she said impatient of his silence and his gaze. 'If you do not intend to come to us, why are you in these woods? Everyone said you were shut up at Willowsleigh, writing, composing, creating, I know not what. What are you doing here, almost disguised?'

'I have been here some days,' replied Syrlin abruptly. 'I have seen you several times, driving with your ladies, riding with your gentlemen. I only came for that. I tell you I should never have made myself known to you but that you were just about to tread where the ice is as brittle as glass, and where I sank up to my hips this morning. You are always surrounded. I never expected to see you like this alone.'

'And why should you want to see me alone?' she was about to say when she remembered the burning words which he had spoken to her on the evening before the Lansmere ball, and which the entrance of her cousin had arrested only half uttered.

Such offence as she had felt at the song of 'La Reine pleurait' arose in her now, and more intensely, yet it was crossed by and fused with a sense of vague and dangerous sweetness, a sudden consciousness of all the heat and strength and magic which passion can lend to life. The directness of his avowals made it impossible to ignore them; he spoke as though it were the most natural thing in life that he should wander, hidden thus, merely to hear the passing sound of her carriage wheels, merely to see the passing shadow of her riding horse!

It was absurd, it was melodramatic, it was like a hero of Hugo's, a lover of Sardou's; it confused her, offended her, violated all her canons of good taste, of prudence, of etiquette; and yet, as she stood there in that wintry loneliness and stillness with those dark eyes pouring down their light upon her, she was moved as Mary Stuart had been moved by Chastelard, and learned that there were other things in life than courts and councils, calm custom and chill routine.

Syrlin perceived that momentary yielding, that softened, hesitating, troubled mood, and a flood of passionate eloquence rose to his lips and spent itself in headlong unmeasured adoration.

He had been many days upon these moors, living hardly, hiding himself from all to whom his features were familiar, brought thither by that hunger of the heart to look on what it loves, which in absence eats away the peace of every true lover. The sudden and unhoped for meeting with her alone by the frozen river mastered his prudence, effaced his fears of alienating her, and destroyed all his self-control. All which had been pent up in his soul through these many lonely months found expression now in that vivid and warmly coloured speech which was so natural to him and of which the ardent accents seemed to change the wintry eve into a tropic day.

Many had been the declarations of hopeless passion to which she had listened, often with slender patience and slight sympathy. But these had been naught beside the worship, the adoration, the humility, the pride, the force, the fervour of this appeal to her which poured out on her the treasures of a heart, virgin in feeling and divine in its ideals.

As she heard, her own heart was stirred to some echo of it, as a lyre long mute will sometimes answer to a master hand. She did not seek to interrupt him: she listened passively, her eyes gazing on the frozen grass against her feet, the colour coming and going in strong emotion beneath her transparent skin.

'You are mad,' she said in a voice which trembled slightly but was not cold or angered. 'You are mad. I am nothing that you think me. What good can such folly do you? What happiness can it bring?'

'Happiness!' he echoed. 'Dearer is torture which comes from you than all the common joys of earth. I love you; I love you; I love you! Do you not understand that it is delight enough merely to say that unrebuked to you?'

'But I do rebuke you,' she murmured, whilst a faint soft smile hovered on her lips, which had grown pale. 'You should not think thus; you should not feel thus; I have told you it is madness.'

The chiding was sweet as the south wind to the ear of Syrlin. It brought to him whispers of all hope, all ecstasies, all fair fruition, as the south wind stirring in the cold of spring brings all the promise of the summer with its breath.

'I live to-day, let me die to-night!' he murmured rapturously, 'If it be madness, it is one that gods might envy. Do you know what it is for me to love you thus? How should you know? The men of your world cannot love. When they think they love, and are repulsed, they buy a new rifle and go where they can kill wild boars or bulls. How should you know what my love is to me? It is the core of my heart. It is the essence of my soul. It is every fibre and nerve of my being given to you. I love you as Dante Beatrice, as Petrarch Laura, humbly, devoutly, ethereally; but I love you also as the eagle loves, as the lion loves, as the man loves when he is outside the deadening influences of the world, fiercely, blindly, idolatrously, exclusively, with rage as well as rapture!'

'Hush, hush!' she said faintly; a vague fear moved her, the first fear she had ever known. Yet something like that dreamy lulling magnetism which it is said comes over those who feel the hot breath of the desert king upon their faces, came over her under the sirocco of this boundless and dauntless passion. He felt his power over her, his eyes flashed fire in the gloom of the twilight, his gaze poured its magnetic forces into hers, his hand stole near her and touched timidly and reverently the furs of her dress.

Alas for him! at that moment the calling of distant voices sounded on the frosty air; her name echoed over the icy wastes and smote his ear and hers.

'Go, go!' she said breathlessly, as she shook him off. 'They have missed me and are coming after me. Go, go! Must I tell you twice? If you are found with me here I will never see you again! You have no right to draw ridicule and misconstruction on me by your follies. The whole world is not a theatre. You must learn to remember that.'

He grew very pale; all the ardent, warm,

melting tenderness which had given such softness and fire to his regard died down as a leaping flame will sink and die in darkness.

'You are afraid!' he cried.

All his features hardened into scorn; he loosed his hold on her and he breathed loudly and with effort; his checked passion choked him, thrown back upon itself like a fiery horse arrested in mid-career.

She turned on him with imperious command and indignation.

'I am afraid of nothing; but I do not choose to be found with you here, like a gamekeeper's wife discovered in an intrigue with a gipsy. Go! I order you, go! If you have any honour in you—go!'

His head dropped under the sting of the last words; with a fierce and bitter oath he turned from her, and, plunging amongst the brushwood of the river-bank, was quickly lost to her sight amongst its brown and tangled undergrowth.

The voices calling on her name drew nearer and nearer.

She paused a moment, drawing a deep long breath to still the beating of her nerves, then she slipped her skates upon her feet and went to meet the persons seeking her.

'Where have you been? We have been frightened out of our wits!' called Lord Glastonbury, who was the foremost of the group of gentlemen.

'Whom were you talking to, Lady Avillion?' cried those behind him. 'We had just despaired of ever finding you above the ice when by good fortune we heard some one speak.'

'It was a stray tourist,' she answered lightly. 'He warned me that the ice of the Swiftsure would not bear. You need not have come after me, my good people. I know my way home.'

Lord Glastonbury looked curiously at her.

'It is odd weather for tourists to be abroad,' he said curtly. 'Surely in common gratitude you offered him a night's rest at Brakespeare?'

'I did not think of it,' she answered indifferently. 'And I am afraid I am never grateful. But I dare say he will sleep quite as soundly at the village inn.'

At the tea hour, when she had come down amongst her ladies, clad in loose flowing folds of silver tissue, the speculations and the mirth were great over what they termed her adventure. She herself said very little, but she looked fatigued.

'Surely the wanderer was Mr. Whistler,' said the Duchess of Queenstown, 'come northward to study a symphony in black and white.'

'It must certainly have been an artist of some sort,' said Avillion with a slight momentary smile, and his eyes under their languid lids turned on his wife. 'I wish you had brought him in,' he added. 'He might have amused us.'

She felt a wave of warmth pass over her face and throat. And a feeling of hatred against Syrlin rose in her and embittered his memory. Yet when later on she took the arm of Lord Greatorex to go in to dinner she thought of him with contrition, alone and out in the snow-storms of the night, or miserably and hardly lodged in some peasant's cabin or some moorland alehouse.

Her dinner table, strewn with white and red roses, illumined by the electric light, glittering with gold statuettes and silver baskets, with its ripple of low voices and amused laughter around it, and its dozen powdered lacqueys behind the chairs, seemed to her an insolent, odious, ostentatious, stupid parade.

Every now and then she met her husband's eyes; they had a mild derision, a subdued triumph in them, which scorched her like the touch of a hot iron.

CHAPTER XLVIII

During the evening Avillion left the drawing-room for a moment and went to his own apartments. He wrote there a few words on a sheet of paper, sealed it, and bade his man send it to the head keeper.

'It would really be amusing,' he thought, 'to have *le beau ténébreux* taken up for poaching and brought before the Bench. Alceste before the great Unpaid would be enchanting.'

But it was not an amusement in which he could indulge, for it would have startled and driven away the offender and delayed that discovery and denouncement which he himself so impatiently awaited. Avillion was no sportsman, but he knew enough of sport to know that you must never alarm your quarry if you would draw near enough to bring it down. Yet he took delight in the belief that her pride had fallen, her dignity succumbed, her strength yielded to mortal frailties, and the desire to know it beyond doubt, to be able to prove and publish it, made him unscrupulous as to any means by which he could secure such testimony.

All evil grows apace, and the acerbity of his feelings against her and his desire to be free of her obliterated in him all those principles of race and breeding which had hitherto restrained and redeemed his character.

All these years he had praised and respected his wife for the prudence with which she had preserved her judgment and borne high his name amidst flattery and provocation of every kind. But now, for the gratification of his own impulses and animosity, he was ready to disgrace his own name in her person.

'Let her go and live with her comedian amongst his Moors and Jews,' he thought, with brutal eagerness to hound out of his world the mother of his heirs. He hated Syrlin, but he hated her much more; and his love for himself and for his own indulgence was greater yet than either sentiment.

In the morning he heard that his orders had been obeyed, that search and inquiry had been made on his lands, and that a foreigner, young, and apparently rich, had been staying at the disused post-house on the moors, and had been frequently seen in the wilder and lonelier parts of the park. The identity of the stranger with Syrlin did not appear to have occurred to any of the men who were employed in his woods and forests, but Avillion from various evidence had no doubt left in his own mind about it.

'A *grande passion* with a vengeance!' he thought in amaze; not even for the Duchess de Charolois would he himself have stayed at a moorland post-house with a peat fire and a flock bed, and frozen land and water all around him,

He had no doubt whatever that the meeting by the Swiftsure had been an intentional one, an appointment interrupted by the accidental interference of Lord Glastonbury. Well, they should meet again, uninterrupted, if they liked! He smiled and wished them joy of their erotics, with the mercury below zero and their *décor de scène* frozen bracken and icicle-hung bushes. All the cruelty which was in his nature, long unchecked by egotism and only covered by a polished manner, awakened and increased in him. He would have exposed and disgraced his wife with delight and without mercy or hesitation.

If his generation and his rank had permitted, he would have treated her with un-

sparing brutality and personal violence. As
he could not do that, he gave her rope and
hoped that she would hang herself!

He observed on the following days that
she made excuse not to leave the house, or
else drove some ladies in her pony sledge and
never was alone. 'This is only a blind,'
thought Avillion, with that sceptical shrewd-
ness which so often overshoots its mark, and
is more mistaken than simplicity. She was
never unaccompanied because she dreaded
such another meeting as that beside the Swiftsure. She knew not whether Syrlin was still
in the north, still on those moors, or whether,
disappointed and repulsed, he had abandoned
his enterprise and left the county.

She had no clear memory of what she had
said herself, only every syllable of his impassioned declarations remained engraven upon
her remembrance.

When he had left her and had plunged
into the blackened and frozen undergrowth
of the larch woods which fringed the Swiftsure, Syrlin had gone on and on, forcing his
way through all obstacles in his path like a
horse broken loose from constraint and blind
with his own excitement. The sound of the
voices of those who joined her coming to him

from the distance on the icy air increased almost to delirium the fever which was upon him. He had come thither on no fixed errand, on no definite scope, merely, as he had told her, because the desire to see her again had become irresistible. It was only when he had left her that the full sense of the danger to her of his concealed presence on her husband's estates was borne in upon him.

The last words which she had spoken showed him the greatness of his fault against her, and the risks to which he had exposed her. He had all the romance of a Rollo, the fervour of a Romeo, but he had nothing of the calculation, nothing of the cruelty, of a libertine.

He adored her as, in the old dramas of history and art, men adored women ; he could never have reached the cynical egotism with which Avillion could plan and trace and compass the seduction of what he admired, with the patience and the circuitous approaches of an engineer laying down the lines of attack which are destined to reduce a city by long siege. His repentance for what he had done was as extreme as his regret and his disappointment as he went over the frozen marshes, often up to his knees in breaking ice and crushing brushwood, whilst the long winter twilight slowly settled into night, and through the silence and darkness there only came the boom of a famished bittern, the bleat of a starving otter. He wandered away from the course of the river and lost his road and all knowledge of where he was. He might have perished miserably in a snowdrift, or fallen in the starless gloom down into some gully or ravine or tarn, had he not met with a sheepdog out searching for his lost sheep. Following the dog he came to the fold, and to the hut of the shepherd close by; and there he stayed until morning. With sunrise he returned to the old disused posting-house upon the Brakespeare moors where his momentary abode had been made, and wrote a letter to her into which all the soul of a poet was poured, and all the desperation of a lover who broke his heart on hers as José upon Carmen's.

With great imprudence he gave this letter to a village boy to be carried to the Castle, and himself took his departure from the north, lest the mad desire to see her face and hear her voice again should be stronger than himself, and again compromise her by some accidental meeting on which some false construction should be placed by others. He knew that he had no right to compromise her; not even such right, if it can be called so, as would have come from that responsive passion which would alone have made courage in such a position incumbent upon her. He was imprudent from temperament, heedless from scorn of conventionality and disdain of caution, impetuous in all moods and phases of feeling, and used from character to underrate the need and the value of all hesitation to obey the dictates of passion. It was as impossible for him to comprehend the temperament and moral atmosphere of such a woman as she was as it would be for a native of the tropics to understand the winter of the poles. Beaufront had warned him long before that such a character as hers would for ever remain unintelligible to him in its self-love, which yet was not selfishness, in its deference to opinion, which yet was not cowardice, in its resistance to impulse, which yet was not heartlessness.

'You are afraid!' he had said to her with cruel scorn, but he knew that he had no title to make it a reproach to her if she were indeed afraid to seem what she was not, afraid to appear to have deserted those laws of custom and of duty to which she had been entirely true. The world was always with her; a rival so potent that he could never hope to vanquish it.

He was but Chastelard: and she, though song might charm her ear, and worship touch her heart, would, he felt, beyond all things never forget, never let him forget, that she was a queen, and he but a minstrel, a lutist, a stringer of rhymes.

Meanwhile the village boy to whom he had given his letter idled on his way, bought food and marbles with the money given him, found playmates to share both, and loitered about the park snow-balling rabbits, so that an under keeper took him rudely to task, and relieving him of the sealed envelope sent him back to his moorland home whimpering and frightened. The under keeper having had secret orders given him by his principal, carried the letter to the head keeper, who in turn carried it to his lord's body servant Phillips.

Avillion took it as if he thought it one of his own, being gravely careful to keep up appearances, although he knew that Phillips was aware of the orders which the keepers had received. Alone he opened the letter and read it.

The contents surprised him. There seemed no possibility of doubting the penitence, the hopelessness, and the unhappiness which breathed in every line.

'Is it possible that he is still only a suitor dolorous and forlorn? I thought him too experienced to waste his time in sighs to the empty air,' he thought, regretful and impatient, as he gave the letter, carefully closed, back to Phillips.

'It is a letter for my lady! You should be more careful,' he said severely. 'Give it to one of her women.'

Phillips, who was far too admirably trained not to fall in with all his master's humours and carry out any pretence which his master liked to fabricate, made profound excuses for his own negligence, and appeared wholly to have forgotten the orders which he had received a few days before.

That evening when she went to her room, before dinner she found the letter lying before her mirror, and at a glance she recognised the frank and careless handwriting which she had seen in the same manner on her table once before when he had sent her the verses on the harvest-mouse.

'Does he even suborn my maids?' she thought with a flush of anger. 'Must he always believe that he is still upon the stage?'

Her pride was offended. She disliked these romantic follies, these secret melodramatic ways.

'Who gave you that letter?' she asked her attendant.

The woman, who was warned by Phillips not to mention himself or his lord, affected, and affected admirably, astonishment and ignorance.

'The letter could not have come here by itself, and no one but you or Marie has put it there,' she said, undeceived by the maid's acting. 'It is a petition, I can see. But whoever has anything to say to me can say it by post.'

She lighted a match and set fire to the letter, which blazed a little and then smouldered into ashes on the china tray where she had laid it to burn. She watched its destruction with a pressure of regret at her heart. Here and there words caught her eye as the fire consumed it, imprudent words, words full of passion and humility, entreaty and despair.

But her soul was shut to his prayers, for her pride was more intense than her emotion. She hated to think that he brought into her life the secret and foolish intrigue of stage-passions, could approach her with the sensational and dramatic action with which in his theatres he had wooed Marguerite, Marion Delorme, Angélique, Doña Sol, Froufrou!

Avillion said that night as Phillips undressed him:

'I hope you were careful to send that packet of my lady's to her rooms?'

Phillips replied with sober countenance, 'I am happy to say it was of no importance, my lord; the women told me it was only a petition, and her ladyship burnt it unread.'

'Unread!' thought Avillion, who felt once more extreme surprise.

Women do not burn letters unread when they come from those whom they love. But as his own inclination and habits were always to scheme, with many involutions and affectations, he concluded, on maturer thought, that this letter had been only a ruse; a letter of fictitious despair, written to put himself off his guard, and burnt by his wife with fictitious indifference for the same purpose.

The extreme finesse of his own mind, and the intricacies of his own actions, disposed him to a view of the motives and acts of others which was, in its manner, often as fallacious and misleading as the impressions and conclusions of an optimist are in another sense. That no one ever took a straight line when they could take a curved one, seemed to him an axiom of human life and conduct.

By that intuition which some women possess, and which knowledge of the world increases, she was sensible that her husband was aware of the visit of Syrlin, and she felt that her guests were by some means all more or less conscious of it likewise. Some of those who had followed her to the Swiftsure had, she imagined, recognised either his voice or his countenance. The knowledge was to the greatest extent irritating to her.

Such a secret known of her seemed to drop her at once to the level of those heroines of scandalous stories whom she had always held in such cold contempt. Her heart hardened more and more against the man who had brought such misconstruction upon her, even whilst more and more the eloquence of his words, the magnetism of his regard, remaining in her memory, awakened in her emotions to which she had all her life been a stranger.

Had she had the power of Mary Stuart, she would unrelentingly have sent him to the scaffold, but she would have suffered more than he when the axe would have fallen.

Syrlin meanwhile had returned to Willowsleigh; and in the long lonely hours which were there his chosen lot he remembered and looked at the verses and scene of his drama which, perfected and polished, and with all his powers concentrated in it, had been finished and put away before he had gone northward.

He had ceased to be able to judge of it. At one moment it seemed to him that he had in it a fair title-deed to more durable fame than that which he had already won; at another it seemed to him vacuous, senseless, mere metre, without a soul in it, mere empty sound which would awaken no human heart to an echo.

'And though it had all Musset's and Shelley's hearts in it, all Swinburne's melody and all Heine's sorrow, what would she think of it or of me?' he said bitterly. 'No more than Mary Stuart thought of Chastelard. Francis is a scrofulous sick boy, Darnley is a vicious fool, Bothwell is a brute: yet all these may mate with her; Chastelard is only a presumptuous mime and must not lift his eyes to her in public!'

Certain of her words had entered into him, and stung his soul as a loaded whip stings the flesh with its strokes.

They had been words in which the instinctive, unconquerable, innate contempt of a great lady for all outside her own pale of birth and of habit had escaped her, being stronger and more enduring in her than any warmth of emotion or sympathy of thought. Though all the world could crown him as Rome crowned Petrarch, it would not make him nearer to her.

The winter days and nights were long and dull and humid in the valley of the Thames; but he remained there alone, denied to all, even almost always to Auriol.

He was a prey to a cruel and insatiable passion, and to a genius which conceived ideals and ambitions such as no reality on earth could satisfy. He was like Faust in the solitude of the mountain, accompanied by Mephistopheles, and tortured by the desire for Helen.

CHAPTER XLIX

WITH the early days of February the long series of winter festivities at Brakespeare drew to a close. The Houses were to assemble in the middle of the month, and Lord Greatorex had expressed his hope to the magnates of his party that they would be in their places on the day of the opening of Parliament. Such demands on self-sacrifice were growing numerous and onerous, but the great personages grumbled and yielded. Avillion, quoting many disquieting precedents from the administrations of Lord Shelburne and Lord North, suffered himself to be drawn to London, and Mme. de Charolois, who found England suit her health, purchased a very pretty house in a corner where the trees and water of St. James's Park made a sylvan landscape in front of the balconies. She was said to be suffering from that vague and elastic malady anæmia, and only one physician, and that a London one, had ever understood her case. It was a gentle and benevolent disease, and never impaired her beauty, interfered with her engagements, or prevented her taking any fatigue which pleased her, but it was always there, extremely useful and exceedingly interesting.

Beaufront was away in the extreme East, yachting, no one knew precisely where, in some Chinese, Siamese, or Burmese waters; and the house in Wilton Street saw him no more, although its doors were open, its furniture uncovered, and the white cat was lying in its old place at its mistress's feet in front of olive-wood fires.

There is something in the routine of habit, the monotony of social rites and seasons, repeating themselves with the regularity of a timepiece, which is in painful and jarring contrast with the capricious leaps and bounds, the fateful uncertain heat and cold, the continual and surprising changes of the moods, the affections, the passions, the sorrows, the joys, of the men and women who are caught in the meshes of this external life which so controls and holds them, whilst their internal life is so varying and changeful. The machinery of society ticks on, rolls to and fro, runs on the same immovable lines, and alters neither for love nor death, and men and women follow it passively, whilst all their souls are dissolved in the acid of grief or turbulently tossed on the waves of desire.

When Freda Avillion descended at her own mansion, and saw all the familiar evidences of the familiar existence, a weariness and sickness came over her, as it comes over the souls of those who return from the burial of their best beloved and see the chair, the pen, the clock, the clothes, all that the dead wore and used, all in their place, intact, untouched, the inanimate things all strong, safe, durable, only the spirit and the heart blotted out and trampled into nothingness.

Something of the sharpness and painfulness of such a contrast jarred on her as she returned to this life of ceremonies, of etiquette, of entertainment, of politics, of incessant movement, which had once seemed to her so all-sufficient, so all-absorbing. Nothing in it was changed; but in her all.

She put the golden yoke upon her shoulders, and trod the velvet-covered treadmill; but that interest and illusion in her social labours which had once existed for her were gone for ever.

Her body came back, and sat and moved,

and curtsied and bowed, and drove and rode; and her face smiled, her voice spoke, her ear seemed to listen, her mind seemed to reply, but her spirit was far away, by the frozen reeds of a river listening to the burning words of a reckless passion.

She remembered every word; she recalled every accent; she could see the light and fire of his eyes pour down on her; and these memories rarely left her. When she sat at great dinners, at long debates, through noisy divisions, at royal supper tables, in the murmur of conversation, in the sound of orchestral or vocal music, she heard always the voice of Syrlin saying, 'I love you as Dante Beatrice, as Petrarch Laura; but I love you also as lions love, as eagles love, as men love!'

She longed for, yet she dreaded, the moment when she should meet him once more in the world.

'Lady Avillion looks ill,' some one said in hearing of the boy Flodden, who had passed his time miserably but honourably, in becoming acquainted with his great estates and his duties to and on them, hoping feverishly all the winter for invitations to Brakespeare which were never vouchsafed to him.

'I cannot have that insufferable lad here,

with his ill-timed adoration,' she had thought when Avillion had suggested asking him.

'They say you are not well—I hope it is not true!' he said timidly to her one night on the staircase of the House of Commons.

'Who says so?' she said angrily. 'No; it is not in the least true; and if it were true, have you studied physic that you should be entitled to ask such a question?'

'I beg your pardon,' he murmured. 'But I thought you did not look so strong as last year, and you seem not to care for things— even for these things—any more.'

He made a movement of his hand towards that body of the House where the unseen representatives of the nation were howling like hyenas, and crowing like cocks, and whooping like red Indians, the echoes of their uproar penetrating to the passages and stairways.

'I certainly do not care for hideous noises, I do not remember that I ever did,' she replied coldly, 'and you will oblige me very much, my dear Lord Flodden, if you will not make my appearance the occasion for your remarks either to myself or others.'

'I beg your pardon,' he said very humbly once more, as he grew red to his eyes with mortification. 'I am afraid that I am so *gauche* and stupid; I offend you always; last year you were so kind to me that—'

'It really makes one resolve never to be kind to anyone,' she said impatiently. 'It is always brought up against one as if one's temporary good-nature gave hostages to eternity.'

'Oh!' said Flodden indignantly, the injustice of such a rebuke stinging into rebellion even his devoted submission. 'Oh! never, never could I think such a thing; I am awkward, and shy, and foolish, I know, but I am not so presumptuous as to—'

'My dear lord,' said his idol very cruelly, 'pray go and talk about yourself to some débutante; your feelings and failings will interest any marriageable young lady immensely, but they do not interest me in the least, and I cannot possibly stay in a very draughty stone passage to hear you expatiate on them. Please see if my servant is below!'

Flodden went, as he was forced to go, down the remaining stairs to the doorway, where her footman was gazing up at the murky skies above the Speaker's Yard, and her horses were fretting and fidgeting in the foggy and heavy night.

The boy's gentle and loyal heart was wounded to the quick. He could make no reply to such an attack, for she told him that every expression of his feelings and opinions wearied her. He realised that he had always been absurd in her sight, and had been only not insignificant because his position made him of political interest and value. Many bitter upbraidings and sarcasms crowded to his lips; but he was a gentleman, and to a woman he could not utter even a truth which was discourteous. He escorted her to her carriage in silence, and drew the soft fur rug over her knees carefully, bending his head low so that she should not see the tears which had started to his eyes. But although long-suffering and chivalrous beyond the majority, and capable of infinite self-abnegation and devotion, he was human, and human passions conquered him for a moment as he closed the door of the brougham, and said, with a sense that in so speaking he was unmanly and revengeful, as he should not have been:

'I suppose you know that a person who had better fortune in your favour than I is lying very ill?—in danger even they say?'

He saw her face change colour quickly, but she remained mistress of herself.

'Of whom do you speak in such a roundabout fashion? Who is it you mean by your euphemism?'

'Syrlin,' said Flodden curtly; then, without another word, fearing wholly to lose his composure if he waited to see the confession of emotion on her features, he turned away and crossed the yard rapidly; her footman mounted the box and her carriage drove away.

She had already given the order for home, as she had to change her dress for a reception.

As Flodden turned away and went with a heavy heart across the Speaker's Yard, he was met, as he had been met in the previous session, by Lorraine Iona, who had been dining at Mr. Peel's house. By the lamplight Iona looked with interest at the young man's face, so sad, so dull, so overshadowed.

'You have everything your heart can wish,' he thought; 'and you are fretting your bonny life away for a woman who only thinks you a tiresome young fool.'

Aloud he said, as he joined Flodden:

'Come out of the beargarden! I was going in, but on second thoughts I will not do so to-night. I will go home instead and re-read Pitt's life, to see once again what a fine figure he cut in adversity, harassed by war, financial strain, and every form of distress; whilst in peace and in prosperity, or what should be prosperity, these men of our time allow strikers to paralyse commerce, and conspiracies to paralyse governments, and muzzle honest dogs whilst they leave blackguard agitators unmuzzled. Will you come home with me?'

'Thanks, no; yes. No, I fear I cannot,' muttered Flodden, who was thinking only of his own utter misery and consuming jealousy.

'Of course you have a dozen engagements, but engagements are oftener thrown over than kept in this impolite world.'

'I don't remember; I was going somewhere,' murmured the youth, looking vaguely around him at the lamps, the policemen, the courtyard.

Iona put his hand on Flodden's arm.

'If it hold so little place in your thoughts it can scarcely be worth keeping. Come and smoke a water-pipe with me.'

'You are very kind,' said Flodden. 'I must bore you infinitely.'

'You do not bore me, and you need not

be afraid of me; I have no daughter whom I want you to marry. Come.'

Flodden, who could never resist the magnetism of this seductive solitary, went with him.

'Why will you stay in this Babylon?' said Iona. 'Babylon, do I say? The name is profaned. Babylon had the glory of cloudless skies, of rushing waters, of palm-groves and rose-gardens, and white roofs glittering in radiant light. Man might there be defiled, though not to such bestiality as here; but there Nature was undefiled—not soaked in poisoned vapours, not choked in filthy soot, not crushed under weight of bricks and iron, and lost in squalor and in horror as here! Why do you stay here? Is there no grove blossoming, no grass growing, no burn flowing anywhere, that you waste the loveliest years of your youth here?'

'I do not know why I stay,' replied the boy. 'I hate it; but it is custom, some say it is duty. You yourself have told me to " study the cities and the minds of men."'

'Yes; but you are in no state to study them. You are absorbed in your feeling for a woman.'

Flodden coloured hotly; but he was too

honest and too simple to make a denial.
'And you are jealous,' continued Iona as they
passed out of the gates. 'You are jealous,
and jealousy is the vitriol of the soul. It is
the most accursed corrosive in human nature.
You are jealous of Syrlin.'

'I have never given you any right to
say so.'

'I have no right to speak at all to you of
your feelings or your actions. But I have
ventured to take the right because you
interest me, and I am, compared with yourself, an old man, and age may presume without offence. I am grieved to see you the
slave of a passion which makes you the jest of
London.'

'No one has any cause to suspect what I
have never confessed or betrayed.'

'My dear Lord Flodden! You betray, you
confess, with every glance which you cast at
your idol. You are ingenuous to credulity.
You wear your heart on your sleeve. You
are wretched, and are unaware that your
wretchedness is the sport and pastime of
others.'

Flodden withdrew his arm from his
monitor's, and his face grew crimson and
sullen.

'I am not sensible that I am ridiculous. I cannot be more so than a man who makes himself notorious in a thousand eccentric and insane ways.'

'Syrlin is one of those to whom the world has always permitted his caprices; and he has in a sense earned his right to adore his lady. People even say that his feelings are returned. I do not believe that they are; because I believe that she is a woman who will never forfeit her position for any passion that any man living could inspire in her. But she has a certain sentiment for Syrlin. For you she has none. She shows unmistakably that you weary her.'

'I do not intrude on her.'

'Perhaps not; but the way you gaze at her is intrusion. You were a political pawn in her hands. She smiled on you to keep you away from the Opposition. As soon as you were gained over to her party you lost all interest for her. You will deem me a brute for telling you this. But everyone has seen it except yourself.'

'Perhaps I have seen it too.'

'If you have, you should have had dignity enough to conceal your position. A man should never allow others to laugh at him.

If she desired your worship,—oh, then disregard the whole world, and wear your stockings cross-gartered if she tell you to do so. But she does not notice you a whit more than Olivia Malvolio.'

Flodden did not speak; his face burned as he walked on sullenly, his eyes cast down, his mouth trembling.

'Am I cruel?' said Iona in his softest, tenderest tones. 'I fear you will think me so, and impertinent likewise. But I cannot see your young and abundant life wasted on a chimera. Mark my words. Lady Avillion may or may not love as other women love; but she will never sacrifice her place to her emotions. If she love Syrlin he is more to be pitied than you are, for she will take his heart only to break it. Position will always have the foremost claim on her. Syrlin should know that, for he knows women profoundly. But he is blind for the moment, since he fervently believes that she loves him.'

Flodden winced as if a hot iron had touched his flesh.

'She does,' he said in a low stifled voice.

'In her fashion,—possibly. But she will sacrifice him to her pride of place. Whilst you—you in the perfection of youth, fortune, and the capabilities of happiness, throw your life away upon a woman who does not even thank you for the sacrifice.'

'We are not masters of our fate,' murmured the boy.

'In a sense we are not; but in a sense we are. We can weed our garden, though we cannot help the seeds let fall in it by blowing winds and flying birds. If you stay on here you will brood on your unhappy passion until you will lose all control over it, and it will lead you where it chooses. If you have courage and resolve enough to leave London now, at once, and throw yourself into the true interests of your life, you will conquer and will, in time, outgrow it.'

'Never,' murmured Flodden.

Lorraine Iona smiled. Not in derision but compassion; he knew how eternal to youth seem its passions and its pain, and how indeed eternal are they, in a sense, since they for ever destroy the bloom, the dawn, the undimmed ecstasy of life.

'Why do you not warn him then, as well as myself?'

'In the fever which Italians call *perniciosa*,' replied Iona, 'there is a stage at which the physician and the friends go away, and close the door, for they have seen death standing at the foot of the bed and can do nothing. Syrlin is in this stage of the *perniciosa*. Your fever is the green sickness of youth: it will pass.'

They passed on in silence through the gas-lit, dusky, noisy thoroughfares, whilst the many wheels rolled and the many feet hurried around them, until they reached Iona's door. On the threshold his companion hesitated; he was offended, humiliated, resentful.

Iona's luminous, meditative spiritual eyes dwelt on the boy's now pale and averted face.

'Come,' he said softly, and he laid his hand on Flodden's shoulder and gently pushed him into the little entrance hall. The lad followed him meekly. For a while Iona did not address him, but busied himself lighting his brass lamp, setting fire to the incense in the brazier, making some sherbet, speaking to his Arab boy. Then for awhile he smoked in silence. Flodden, refusing the nargileh placed by him, sat with his head buried in his hands, his form shrunk and drawn together as though he had suddenly grown old. 'She loves him!'—that was the one idea dominant to his imagination, clinging to him like the claws of some wild bird. At last Iona, after gazing at him for some time, spoke.

'I was going to Syria next week. My business here is done. I am sick of the hurly-burly, of the hypocrisy, of the everlasting strife and muddle, of the grinding tyranny of trumpery bye-laws, of the coarseness and triviality of social life and its gigantic and unchallenged lies. I am thirsty for a sky without furnace-smoke, for a soil without tramway lines, for a people without a Press, for a world where there is still days undimmed and nights unbroken by the reek and the jar of " civilisation." After a year of Europe I am sick for my Cathay. Tennyson did not know the charm of Cathay. And you?'

Flodden did not reply; he did not move. He sat huddled together and miserable, without a word or a sign in reply.

'You must not come to Cathay,' continued Iona. 'You have possessions and privileges: obligations go with them. You know nothing of your own lands, of your own people. What if you learned to live on them, and amongst them, as no one of your class ever does do nowadays? Before you vote on the land question, study the soil. Before you espouse a party, understand a nation. Go to Bræ-eden, and live there a year, two years, three. Your books by night and your moors by day will teach you what London cannot. Have you courage to accept that life?'

Flodden was still silent.

'Would it be too hard for you? Too near to her? Too close to this wanton, Society, which is for ever after you, as Phædra was after her stepson? Then come away with me to the East, where you shall live on the fruits and roots of the earth, and the water which springs from the rocks. Come with me for a while, to realise how false, how vulgar, how trivial, how burdensome a thing science, and politics, and wealth have made of human life. Come with me where you can see the face of the sky as David and Isaiah saw it, where the stench and the groan of engines are unheard, and the sun rises and sets in pure ether, and physiology has not taught man to tremble lest death should lurk in every hum of a gnat, and to live in ghastly fear with eyes fastened on his own navel. Come away with me to the East, which was the fountain of life, the cradle of religion; come with me and I will teach you how few are the real needs of the body, how boundless is the vision of the soul. Come!'

His eyes shone, his voice was sweet with a strange melody and seduction; he stretched out his hands to the youth, and Flodden yielded to the spell. He rose and put his hands in those of Lorraine Iona.

'I will come with you where you will. Whether to Bræ-eden or to Palestine,' he said. 'Only do not leave me alone. Teach me to forget myself; to live for others.'

'Live first with Nature,' said the teacher. 'She will lead you as the shepherd leads the lamb to the peace of the fold in the hills.

> Nature never did betray
> The heart that loved her; 'tis her privilege
> Through all the years of this, our life, to lead
> From joy to joy: for she can so inform
> The mind that is within us, so impress
> Wit, greatness, and beauty, and so feed
> With holy thoughts, that neither evil tongues,
> Rash judgments, nor the sneers of selfishness,
> Nor greetings where no kindness is, nor all
> The dreary intercourse of daily life,
> Shall e'er prevail against us, or disturb
> Our cheerful faith that all which we behold
> Is full of blessings.'

The very melodious voice of Iona spoke the lines of the great poet of Nature with reverent and tender utterance.

'That is a noble passage,' he said more lightly, 'despite its faulty use of the demonstrative pronoun as a relative, and the (I am sure) typographical error of *wit* for *with*. Write it down on the first page of your book of life.'

'Stay with me,' said the youth, humbly and brokenly. 'Stay with me, or I shall blot and deface those pages. Nothing—no living creature—is true to me except the stray dog which I took from the streets!'

'I will stay with you,' replied Lorraine Iona.

CHAPTER L

'Bring me the evening papers,' said Freda, as she went to her own rooms. But she looked in vain in them for the name of Syrlin; he was no longer an idol of the hour, he had been out of sight for six months, and journalists had in vain rung at the gates of the avenue and forced the chain across the backwater. Such things are not forgiven by those strange awarders of the laurel who call themselves the Fourth Estate.

If only Beaufront had been there! To him alone she could have spoken. But he was away on the Indian Archipelago or the Chinese rivers; and she could think of no one to whom she could apply for information without incurring either risk or ridicule.

It was evident, by the fact that no one had mentioned this thing before her, that all her friends were aware of the interest which it would have for her. She had her clothes changed, some jewels put on, and went to a gathering of notable persons at Shropshire House.

There are few things in life more painful than to go out into the world for sake of hearing confirmed that fear which is harrowing our hearts in its uncertainty; to smile and talk, and flirt and gossip, with the whole of our being strained in horrible tension to catch the first murmur of that which we are dreading to hear, and are thirsting to refute. But she heard nothing.

Even she, who knew the world so intimately, did not wholly realise its extreme heartlessness, its complete and unsparing application to its idols of the merciless law, 'Out of sight, out of mind.'

Syrlin was a great genius; yes, that no one would have denied, but he had chosen to withdraw himself into solitude; the world revenged itself, and effaced his name from its tablets.

Only a few months before, all these people who were about her had talked of nothing but of him, had crowded about him, had cited his words of gall as if they were of honey, struggled to catch his glance, to wake his smile, hung on his accents, and quarrelled for his praise; and now he was lying in suffering, perhaps in danger, within a few miles of them, and no one of them cared!

Yet since the boy Flodden knew it, his illness must, she felt, be generally known.

She saw her husband at the assembly; it was his sister's house, and Avillion, like most proud and egotistical persons, was very careful to honour members of his own family in public, however much he snubbed and avoided them in private. This evening he looked morose; he also had heard of the illness of the man whom he detested, and it caused him serious annoyance. It was not the move he wanted; he desired events to go on more quickly, and all sickness creates an inevitable pause, checks passion, muzzles enmity, and arrests the course of circumstances; it is second only in its numbing influences to its great companion death.

A man who lies on a sick bed is momentarily like a dead man; he is sacred, he cannot be molested or arraigned.

During the evening, Avillion drew near his wife, admired the hibiscus flowers with which her gown was ornamented, and said to her with his slow derisive indolent smile:

'So *le beau ténébreux* is laid low in his Thames marshes. What could he expect after his mad pilgrimage to your shrine? You should have had him openly at Brakespeare; you could not have had any doubt of the cordiality of my hospitality even to those who rejected it.'

She looked him full in the eyes.

'I should perhaps have doubted the motives of your hospitality.'

Avillion raised his eyebrows.

'You have never been just to me,' he said simply, with admirably acted sincerity, so admirably acted that the doubt assailed her as to whether she had indeed been mistaken in her condemnation and construction of him.

In many ways her intelligence was superior to his, but in finesse he distanced her by many a rood; her mind, naturally direct and candid, was no match for the intricate subterfuges and circumlocutions of his own.

'You should certainly pay him a visit,' he added. 'He must have contracted this malady at that wretched little posting-house on the moors.'

Despite her self-control, she felt that her cheeks and throat for a moment grew rose-red as the hibiscus flowers which she wore. She had not previously supposed that her husband had possessed any certainty of his presence at Brakespeare.

Avillion did not appear to notice her emotion, he nodded with a pleasant smile and went on amongst the crowd, stooping his handsome head now to this lady and now to that, and so arriving with no perceptible effort or *empressement* at Mme. de Charolois' side. Long exercise in them had taught him perfection in all such polished manœuvres.

No word except from him did she hear that evening on the subject of her anxiety.

It was not that people were unaware of, or uninterested in it, but that no one had the audacity to speak to her of one who was generally considered in society to be more intimate with her than was acknowledged.

'Why was not Beaufront here!' she thought.

She had never before appreciated the value of that honest, constant, and loyal devotion to her interests which had so often seemed to her interfering or inopportune.

Auriol, whom earlier she could have asked for news of his friend, she could not now address, because since her knowledge of his pretensions to Ina d'Esterre she had treated him with the most marked coldness. Those innocent and timid affections had found neither toleration nor compassion in her. There was therefore no one of whom she could ask or obtain the intelligence which it was evident was known to the town, although not to herself.

'Give me the newspapers of the week,' she said to her attendants when she returned home again.

The journals were sought for in the rubbish-room to which they had been consigned, to be sold afterwards as waste paper by the servant whose perquisite they were, and were brought to her at two o'clock in the morning, when she had been at home about half-an-hour.

Looking over them she found at last the announcement for which she sought; the record, with no details attached, that Syrlin was lying ill at his house of Willowsleigh from rheumatic fever due to exposure to damp and cold.

The time was so short since his sojourn on the Brakespeare moors that she had no doubt her husband had been right in saying that the malady had been contracted there.

How he must rage and fret and chafe! poor chained lion, poor caged eagle!

She could not picture his intense life, his

wild ardours, his impetuous youth, his almost omnipotent powers, thrown down on a sick bed, reduced to the impotence of illness, the helplessness of feeble and stiffened limbs, the sad, tiresome, weary dependence on the care and the pity of others.

She was too wary to be misled by Avillion's careless suggestion that she should pay a visit to Willowsleigh. Even whilst he had momentarily made her think that she might have done him injustice, she was on her guard against all his apparent good-humour and confidence. Her heart ached with regret and anxiety; if she could have taken all Syrlin's physical suffering upon herself she would have done so; but to do that which would have consoled him at the cost of forfeiting her position never occurred to her as possible. He loved her greatly; his passion awoke in her emotions to which she had been a stranger all her life; but to compromise herself for his sake; no, that was beyond her.

It was not virtue which held her back; it was pride. She could not give such a story to the laughter of her world; she could not give such weakness to the irony and the enmity of her lord.

In the presence of Syrlin, under the

magnetism of his intense passion, of his witching eloquence, her soul acknowledged his power, and her spirit soared on the wings he lent to her into an ether of sympathy and desire in which the ambitions and possessions of ordinary life were momentarily as dross and as dust. But in his absence these regained all their hold on her; they could not content her, they had ceased even to please her, but she could not resign them; they had been hers too long.

The pale wintry London sun came through her windows, and found her lying sleepless on her bed; she had not slept at all; she could not banish the picture which fear and fancy drew for her of Syrlin suffering and helpless on his couch of pain, with his dulled eyes strained and open, and his dry lips perhaps muttering delirious phrases and useless appeals to herself.

Perhaps he had not even Auriol beside him.

He had chosen to dwell of late in a rigid and fantastical solitude, and friends require few incentives to withdraw themselves from a joyless life.

'Friendship!' she thought bitterly; 'it is like our loves, our duties, our politics, our religions, our philanthropies, everything that we profess in these days—a mere time-serving shibboleth!'

The morning had many engagements; she took her children to the trooping of the colours before St. James's; she received the d'Orléans family at luncheon; she went to a charitable committee of which she was the head; she took Ina d'Esterre with her to see some pictures and to hear some music; and all these things went on for her as if they were parts of a panorama before which she was seated, looking on at them all and having no share in any of them.

At luncheon the illness of Syrlin was spoken of and regretted by one of the French princes who was his neighbour.

'But I suppose it is nothing serious,' she said with indifference. 'I should think he was very strong.'

'He is strong no doubt,' replied her guest. 'But it is with strong men that illness often goes hardest; and he has been used to warm climates and dry air. The snows and fogs of these isles are death to him.'

'Why would he stay in them?' she said impatiently. 'He has houses elsewhere; and all the world before him.'

'Each of us has all the world before him,' said the gentleman smiling. 'But "Beauty draws us with a single hair," and fastens us down by it, very often in the last place on earth which is good for us.'

'I dare say he went out in flooded fields without fishing-boots,' said the slow soft voice of Avillion from the other side of the table.

Her brother was lunching there also that day. When her guests were gone she went up to him.

'Fulke, go yourself down to Willowsleigh,' she said suddenly. 'You know that M. de Syrlin saved my life at great risk to himself: surely we ought to make some sign—'

Fulke Damer looked embarrassed and sullen; he fidgeted about a little and then replied in the negative.

'I couldn't do it, you know,' he said sulkily. 'People talk. You made yourself conspicuous.'

'I!'—her eyes flashed fire. 'I am rendered conspicuous,' she added, 'when my family persists in ignoring and insulting a person to whom I owe much.'

'Uther asked him down to Brakespeare and he would not go,' said Damer feebly; he himself knew nothing of what he was talking about, and was merely repeating in ignorance what his wife had told him to say.

'In that I presume he followed his own inclinations,' she answered. 'There is no law, that I know of, to compel people to accept invitations.'

'But when they refuse them, they should not hang about the place mysteriously like poachers,' said her brother, with some timidity as to the result of his reply.

'I agree with you that they should not,' said Freda coldly and curtly; and she abandoned the subject.

Why, oh why, she thought with ever-increasing irritation, had he placed her and himself in a false position by that secret and insane visit to the north? It was impossible to explain it; it was as impossible to defend it. No doubt he had expected to be able to preserve a complete incognito, forgetful, or ignorant, of the battalions of keepers and underlings who guard even the outlying portions of English estates, and the curiosity and comments to which the arrival of a stranger gives rise even in the most secluded hamlet. She understood and believed how his romantic and impassioned temperament led him in blind impulse into the wintry wastes around Brakespeare, solely, as he had said, in the desire of seeing her pass by him, of hearing her voice from a distance, of listening to the wheels of the carriage which bore her: but who, even if such a thing could be said, and it could not, who would ever believe that he had been drawn thither by anything less than an assignation with herself? She could certainly have given him up to ridicule had she been base enough for that, but she was base in nothing: she was always generous and always loyal, if seldom compassionate, and he had placed her in a position in which she was compelled to accept and suffer from appearances which were wholly false. A woman more tender of heart would have forgotten because she would have forgiven that; his offence would have been drowned in the vast ocean of his love; but she neither pardoned nor forgot it, she was loyal to him, but she was implacable to him. He must learn, she told herself, that she was not one of the heroines of Dumas or of Sardou, to be adored with headlong folly, and to be drawn into false positions and hidden embraces.

And yet a consciousness of cowardice tormented her, mixed with the intense disquiet which the thought of his certain illness, of his possible danger, awakened in her.

He had not thought twice before he had flung himself between her and that howling multitude, and she was afraid of meeting the derisive smile of a polished society, the petulant censure of her own relatives!

There is nothing so painful to a courageous temper as to be driven into positions in which repression of courage is imperatively necessitated. The bland yet meaning regard of Avillion dared her to be courageous; and she knew that if she were so she would play into his hands.

The days which followed were the most painful of her life.

The public news of Syrlin was varied and contradictory. Some said that he was in great danger; some that he was convalescent; no two reports were unanimous, and the papers, their reporters being still regularly excluded from Willowsleigh, now vied with each other in creating exaggerated and sensational accounts of his sufferings and anecdotes of the manner in which his malady had been contracted.

Amongst all this verbiage, talked and written, she gradually gleaned two facts: one

that his illness must have been caused by his
exposure to the weather on the Brakespeare
moors; and the other that he was extremely
ill indeed. He had never been ill in his life
since the seizure which had followed on his
interview with his father in the forest of
Ellœuf; and the present prostration of his
strength was great in proportion to his long
immunity from the woes of the body.

Every moment some despatch, some note,
some word overheard, some paragraph in a
newspaper, might tell her the worst that she
dreaded to hear; and yet she could ask nothing,
could do nothing, could think of nothing, which
it could satisfy her to do or say. She felt
that all her people, all her world, were waiting
with cruel curiosity to see her give any sign of
anxiety or of weakness; and that knowledge
braced her to a stoical apathy.

'Damnation! I do believe that she does
not care a straw after all!' said her husband
to himself, chagrined and irritated. What
queer creatures women were, he thought. Give
them their heads and they stood stock still!—
rein them in, and they threw up their heels
all over the pasture!

CHAPTER LI

One day Freda saw Ina d'Esterre sitting before her pianoforte with idle hands and bent head, an open letter on her lap.

'Motionless before your music score! What can be the matter?' said Freda as she passed her.

There were tears in the girl's eyes as she raised them.

'M. de Syrlin is in great danger,' she said in a low unsteady voice.

'Is he? Who tells you so?' asked Freda, sensible of the unnatural hardness of her own voice as she spoke.

The girl blushed, and looked down upon her letter.

'Ernst says so—he is with him.'

'Ernst—who?'

'M. Auriol.'

'He writes to you?'

Ina d'Esterre lifted her head with pride

and her eyes glowed brightly through the tears in them.

'Why should he not?' she said in firm tones.

'Why! Because we have forbidden him; because it is intolerable, insolent, dishonourable; because he must not and shall not address you; because he shall never be permitted to abuse his admission into our acquaintance by the injury of our children. It is our own faults; we caress and flatter and fool these artists until they lose all remembrance of what they are and whence they came. It is infamous in him to address a young girl like you as though he were on an equality with you—'

'He is not on an equality with me. He is far above me,' said Ina, rising from her seat and holding her letter to her heart. All her shyness and docility were gone; she was roused like a doe at bay.

'Where have you learnt that jargon?' said Lady Avillion harshly. 'It is jargon. It is not reason. It is not common-sense. He is not one of us. He cannot approach you seriously. It is therefore the height of dishonour for him to endeavour to entangle your ignorance.'

'He is incapable of dishonour,' said the girl bluntly; all her timidity and deference melted in the fires of her indignation.

Then her young heart misgiving her that she had been rude and presumptuous, and her long habits of admiration and obedience recovering their supremacy, she clasped her hands in timid appeal and looked up wistfully into Freda Avillion's face.

'O Aunt Freda! he loves me and I love him. What is wanted more than that? And we shall always be true to one another,—always, always,—no matter what happens in the future.'

Freda put her aside with an unkind gesture.

'You are raving. You dream of impossibilities. There are other things in life than these follies born out of duets and propinquity. All girls have such fancies, and marry all the same someone suitable who is found for them. You will marry Lord Woodbridge, and Auriol will marry some German Elsa or Iseulte who will interpret Wagner to his liking. He has strangely forgotten, and so have you, that you are a minor and a ward of Lord Avillion's. Give me that letter.'

'No,' said Ina steadily. 'I will destroy it if you like; I know every word of it.'

'Give it to me. I am in authority over you.'

Without another word the girl kissed the letter; then tore it into little pieces. So was it safe from all curious eyes and profane hands.

'Ina! what has come to you?' said Freda in amazement. 'I do not recognise you. A child so yielding, so submissive, so dutiful! Has this man bewitched you?'

The girl made no reply.

Deep anger and amazement held the elder woman dumb for a few moments; she could not believe that such an instantaneous transformation could be wrought by a mere sentiment in so young a girl. And beneath her offence and her astonishment was a keener, crueller, more personal, more intense anxiety; she could not see Auriol's letter or know what it said of Auriol's friend. She regretted too late that she had not been gentler with this child, had not endeavoured to win her confidence and gain her sympathies. It was too late; for she could not recede from the position which she had taken up; she could not descend from her pedestal and say to the young girl, 'I am thirsting to hear what you know.'

She had derided, condemned, censured,

insulted, this innocent and harmless love. What was her own? What title had she to upbraid so furiously a sentiment which, however misplaced, was open as the day and full of faith and courage? And was it even misplaced? It was only the canons of an artificial world which could call it so.

Ina d'Esterre saw something of the troubled emotions which were agitating one whom she had ever seen, and deemed, far above all troubles of the heart or any share in human weaknesses. All the immense affection and reverence which she had so long felt for her uncle's wife came back in a flood of tenderness over her. She knelt down at Freda's feet and laid her fair head caressingly against her arm.

'Forgive me if I were rude,' she murmured. 'But I would brave the whole world to do honour to him. And oh, Aunt Freda, he is so unhappy! His friend is so ill.'

For an instant the lips of Freda Avillion trembled as she heard, and she clenched her teeth to keep back the questions which she was longing to ask.

But she remained mistress of herself, and withdrew gently but coldly from the girl's clinging caress.

'You will see your unwisdom, my dear, with time,' she said; 'meanwhile I absolutely forbid you to correspond with anyone unknown to me, and I shall take care that your correspondent is warned not to repeat such imprudence. You are under age and under tutelage, and if he attempt to go against our wishes the law will punish him for *détournement de mineure.*'

With those chill and unkind words she bade the girl rise, and herself left the music-room without any softer speech or gentler glance.

Ina d'Esterre, left alone, stooped for the little fragments of the torn letter and gathered them up tenderly, and put them in the bosom of her frock. Then she stood awhile with her arms leaning on the pianoforte and her chin resting upon her hands. Her young face was very resolute.

'How I pity her!' she thought. 'Oh, how I pity her! She has never loved anyone!'

The proud woman whom she pitied went to her own apartments with an aching and oppressed heart. All things seemed confused and clouded in a world which had once been so clear and so plain to her; and she had a sick, passionate sense that life would be for ever over for her if Syrlin passed from the ranks of the living. She was pitiless to his declarations, she was intolerant of his imprudence, she was afraid of his adoration; but he was nevertheless dearer to her than any human being had ever been.

And Auriol, who wrote from his bedside, said that it was more than possible that he might not live! If her husband had not bade her go thither she would on the instant have ordered out her horses and have gone to Willowsleigh. But the memory of Avillion's smile was always with her like a rankling sliver of broken glass in a wound. Let him triumph? Never, never, never! she said in her soul. Let Chastelard perish unpitied sooner than the pride of the queen be for an instant abased!

CHAPTER LII

THE youth and the strength of Syrlin triumphed over the severity of the malady. After weeks of suffering, and still more tedious days of weakness, he was restored to health, and saw the pale spring sun find out the primroses about the roots of the old trees of Willowsleigh.

'It is good to be alive!' he said with revived gladness in his eyes as he looked, for the first time since his seizure, across the grey wind-blown river and the hurrying clouds of a dull soft sky. Life was pain, desire, fever, longing, but it was also hope; he remembered the yielding sweetness in her rebuke, the troubled softness in her face, as she had listened to him amongst the frozen rushes.

His illness had not impaired his beauty. In the thinness of his face his eyes looked immense; under the transparent skin the blood came and went visibly; his features were spiritualised and seemed illumined as if by some light from within.

'If you do not go into warm air you will die of decline,' said one of the men of science who had attended on him.

Syrlin shook back his clustering hair, and smiled slightly:

'I am tougher than you think. But *che sarà, sarà!*'

He felt as though like Orpheus he had come back from the land of death and shadows. Only one thing had he, Orpheus-like, brought with him: his love for a woman. Neither unkindness nor neglect could destroy it in him: neither scorn nor ingratitude could slay it. All through the darkness of pain and exhaustion he had thought only of her. Awaking to new life as the earth awoke beneath the winds of spring, he thought also only of her.

And yet she had not come once! A stronger rival than any mere mortal held her from him: the many-tongued, hydra-headed, impalpable, intangible, omnipotent entity which men call the world.

'But I will be stronger than the world one day: one day her whole soul shall be mine,' he thought, with that indestructible trust in its own force which is the characteristic at once of love and of genius.

Although he had bitterly upbraided her for her coldness and her calmness, he altogether failed to measure the extent to which she was sufficient to herself; the intense anxiety which ruled her, never to be pitied, never to be ridiculed, never to lose one inch of her dignity and her authority.

He, like Chastelard, could not realise that to such women as she the joys of love can be but mere momentary dalliance; power and dignity are their Alpha and Omega of life.

He did not know, he could not ask, whether she had given him any sign of remembrance throughout these many weeks, and Auriol, who had never left him, volunteered no information. There were many heaps of cards and unopened notes lying where they had accumulated in his antechamber. He turned them over anxiously, but he saw nothing which spoke of her.

He smiled a little bitterly.

'*La Reine n'a pas pleuré!*' he muttered.

'Was I ever delirious?' he asked of Auriol. 'Did I say anything foolish or wild?'

'At times,' Auriol replied evasively. 'But I took care that no one else heard.'

Syrlin coloured like a woman.

'Forget what you heard,' he said abruptly.

'I have already done so,' replied Auriol.

Syrlin sighed. 'Dear friend, have patience with me. I owe you very much. Tell me of your own story. Does all go well with you?'

'In a sense, yes; but not in all.'

'What do you mean?'

'I mean that my sweet child is true to me, and will I think be true. But who can be sure of the stability of a heart of eighteen? And they forbid me all communication with her.'

'Who do?'

'Her people. She is a ward of Lord Avillion's. It seems that the law is with him. She is a minor.'

'What has he said to you?'

'Himself nothing. He has addressed me and menaced me through his lawyers. I am beneath his direct notice.'

'And she—his wife?'

'Nothing; but Ina wrote me that Lady Avillion takes the same side, the same view, as her husband. It is inevitable. From their aspect of life it is entirely natural. It is even their duty to act as they do.'

Syrlin's face darkened with a stormy shadow.

'It is an insult to me. You are my dearest friend.'

'Oh no, you do not enter into it. They do not mean to insult anyone. They do their duty as they see it to a high-born girl whose interests are entrusted to them. They will speak very pleasantly when they meet me, I make no doubt, and will send me a large cheque if I ever sing for them.'

'You accept an outrage as tamely as that?'

'It is not an outrage. It is an inevitable result of my own vanity in supposing that because, as you said once, I dined with them, stayed with them, laughed with them, I was ever one of them. It is the punishment we all receive and deserve when we forget that as art is only the handmaid, so the artist is only the valet, of Society!'

'*You*—say that!—'

'It is not I who say it. The world says it and makes us feel it.'

'You are too humble; such humility is degradation.'

'It is not humility at all,' said Auriol with a fleeting smile. 'I recognise a fact.

What is the use of being blind to fact? In myself I believe that I am the equal of Lady Ina, and I have wherewithal to maintain her in comfort and elegance, though not in splendour. Her tastes are mine, her heart is mine. I believe that she would be happy with me. But the Avillions think otherwise. They consider me utterly inferior to her, and if society were put to the vote it would say that they were right and I a most presumptuous fool.'

Syrlin said no more. His face darkened and his brows frowned.

'Your heart is set on this matter?' he said abruptly. 'Your happiness depends on it?'

'Entirely,' replied Auriol. He was a man of few words. 'It would not matter much what I might suffer; but I think—I believe that she would suffer too. She has no sympathies with the world in which she lives, and her character is serious and very loyal.'

He turned to the music-stand on which some new scores of his own were lying, and said no more.

Syrlin also was silent, but he thought 'Happy are the simple in heart whose loves are innocent as the children who will play about their knees!'

A few days later he went out into society, where he was welcomed with enthusiasm as one restored from the grave, and also as one whose invitations, and whose acceptance of invitations, were ardently coveted. He knew the value of that fervent welcome, and received it with that smile which the most stupid and the least observant felt like the stinging lash of a silken whip.

He knew the world as Richard the Second knew his greyhound.

On the second evening of his reappearance he met Lady Avillion for the first time. He bowed low, but did not approach her.

She hesitated a little while, feeling that the eyes of the courtly crowd around were turned upon her: it was at Lansmere House. Then with a gracious movement she approached him and said with just sufficient warmth to appear natural:

'I am so glad to see you amongst us once more. Are you wholly recovered? All the world was very anxious.'

Syrlin did not reply. He only bowed again very low. His features were pale and cold; to her conscience his eyes seemed to say to her what his lips had said by the frozen reeds of the Swiftsure: 'You are afraid!'

The press of a great reception separated them; she passed on, taking the arm of a Viceroy of India. To those who had seen and heard her, it had seemed the gracious recognition of a great lady who did not forget her debt to him. To him it seemed the intolerable insolence, the cynical patronage, of a woman who knew that every fibre of his heart and soul was hers, yet who chose to see in him only a social inferior.

An insane longing thrilled through him to seize her in his arms, and tear her jewels off her, and carry her away from all this world which absorbed her, as men in the lands where he was born still throw women across their saddle and ride with them far and fast to a camel-hair tent of the desert.

His eyes, so large, so sombre, so brilliant, with the fires of repressed passion burning through their darkness, followed her, and drew her gaze to them and haunted her with their reproach and their scorn. An uneasy vague terror of what he might do, what he might say, pursued her; she felt herself in the presence of a power which she might be powerless to hold in check. All her delicate weapons, of tact, of offence, of disdain, of repression, which were sufficient to restrain the conventional emotions of the men of her world, were impotent to make any impression on the fierce strong pride, and the impetuous vehement emotions, of this nature on which civilisation had so little real empire.

'You are afraid!' His tongue did not say the words again, but she knew that his gaze said it, that his thoughts repeated it. Yes, she was afraid; afraid of him, afraid of herself.

Lovers of formula would have called this fear virtue; but she who trembled under it knew that it was nothing better than all other fear; that is, was a cowardice and an egotism. He had risked his life for her without a moment's thought; and she had let him lie through many weeks of suffering without even a word written or spoken from her. She felt that he had the right to scorn her; and this scorn hurt her, made her shrink from herself.

The beauty of his face, spiritualised and transfigured by suffering, the scorn of his blazing eyes, seen suddenly and thus amongst a fashionable crowd, after long weeks of silence and separation, gained a power over her which he had never possessed before.

'Is this love?' she thought, startled, incredulous, indignant with herself, thrusting away in vain an instinct which was stronger than herself, and of which she could not comprehend the nobility or the force.

Love had always seemed to her a mere emotional weakness or physical indulgence. Was she at heart no better, no higher, no stronger than those women of the theatre, those heroines of dramatic verse, whom she had so long despised, with whom she had so violently forbidden him to number her?

Later in that evening, at Lansmere House, Syrlin led Ina d'Esterre aside for a moment, unobserved, to a little alcove filled with flowers at some distance from the reception and ball-rooms, where the press of the greatest crowd was.

'Lady Ina,' he said abruptly, 'will you have strength and courage to be true to my friend?'

She was startled, she coloured to her eyes.

'Has he told you?' she said tremulously.

'He has told me all,' said Syrlin. 'He will wait for you for years like Jacob. But you—you are so young, you are in the midst of the world of false forms and false measures; will you be true to him?'

'Yes.'

It was only one word, spoken very low, but she looked up in his face as she spoke, and he saw that it was a vital truth, a promise which she would never break.

'That is well,' he said gently. 'He is worthy of your constancy and of your courage. Both will be tried, I fear.'

He paused; then added with an effort:

'Lady Avillion has no sympathy with you, no forgiveness?'

Ina shook her head.

'She only sees as society would see,' she answered. 'She does not understand. She has never cared greatly for anyone.'

'There would be no possibility of changing her views?'

'Oh, no; none. She is--she is—you know, so very noble and generous and kind in many ways, but she cannot see that feeling matters, that sympathy is happiness, that separation is suffering.'

'She is too great a lady!' said Syrlin bitterly. 'Goddesses do not need common human food. They live on the nectar of their own perfections. Listen, Lady Ina; you know little of me, but Auriol will tell you that whatever faults I have, and I have many, I can be a true friend. I am his, I will be yours if I can. An affection innocent and noble like his and yours should not be broken by the cloven hoof of worldly considerations. Trust me and I will do what I can.'

'I do trust you, for he loves you dearly,' said the girl with simplicity and feeling. She put out her hand to Syrlin, and he raised it reverentially to his lips.

'I salute Auriol's wife,' he said gently as he did so.

At that moment Freda passed the entrance of the little room. She was conversing with Lord Greatorex, but her glance—swift, curious, angered, astonished—swept like azure lightning over the two who stood there amongst the glories of the scarlet and orange-coloured orchids. She did not pause, nor did she break off her conversation, but her heart leapt within her with a leap of jealousy like a lioness's rage.

That child!—who had nothing but her hazel eyes and her wild rose like skin!—what could he see in her, what could he say to her, why should he kiss her hand with such emotion?

She remembered Auriol; she supposed that they might be drawn together by that common sympathy; she recalled Syrlin's plead ings in favour of his suit, and his bitter ironies on the views of the world : still the sight of him beside the girl Ina was offensive to her, suspicious to her. Should he who loved herself even have eyes to see or ears to hear that such a child existed ?

All the exactions, all the tyrannies. all the exclusiveness which accompany love, when it is awakened at all in women such as she, sprang into existence in her, and were cruel, dominant, unreasoning, as such feelings ever are.

Ina, when they drove homeward, felt the glacial coldness of her manner, heard the chilling tacit rebuke of her brief good-night; but the girl believed that her displeasure was caused by the remembrance of Auriol, and asking no questions, she went to her own room in resignation, and said her prayer at her bedside with hope and confidence, begotten by the promise and the confidence of Syrlin.

'We shall be happy some time,' she thought with all the trustfulness of youth as she fell asleep, whilst the waking birds in the gardens of Avillion House sang little trills of song amongst the budding hawthorns and the brown shoots of the elm-tree branches. In Lady Ina's youthful belief, genius was a deity, and had deity's omniscience and omnipotence. The estrangement from her of the woman whom she admired and adored was pain and sorrow to her; but it had no power to weaken her loyalty to her word, or affect her devotion to the man to whom she held herself betrothed.

'Children are always inconstant,' Freda Avillion had said with contemptuous disbelief in the resisting forces of youth; but Ina d'Esterre was a woman in feeling, and one of those women in whom tenderness is as long-lived as it is innocent and unselfish in its substance.

Her elder, meanwhile, found no rest at all; but wide awake heard the twittering of the birds with the impatience of insomnia, and watched the flame of her night lamp, pale in the morning sunshine, with sleepless eyes.

For the first time in her whole existence she was a prey to those emotions which she had always considered as the degrading insanity of the senses, as the absurd violence of ill-regulated natures in those whom she had always implacably ridiculed and condemned.

CHAPTER LIII

THE day after their meeting at Lansmere House Syrlin sent out invitations to all the great world of London and Paris for an evening party at Willowsleigh in a month's time. In the corner of the cards was the single word *Représentation*.

It was soon rumoured that the evening was to witness the representation of 'Le Glaive' in his own theatre, he himself acting in the chief rôle. It was known that he was the author of the drama, and that it was written in verse; the music of the songs in it having been composed by Auriol. Curiosity was extreme, and expectation intense.

He had withdrawn from the stage and from the world. The desire to see him return, if but for a night, to both, became as ungovernable as it was universal in society.

In those autumnal months of absolute seclusion which had preceded his imprudent sojourn on the Brakespeare moors, he had brought his work to the utmost lyric and dramatic perfection, and he had prepared for it all that material assistance which is necessary to place the life of a drama in action before its spectators. The first artists of Paris only needed a word from him to crowd to his call, and his own knowledge and experience made easy to him the arrangement of all those practical details and effects which no poet can afford to esteem lightly in the scenic preparation of his creation. He had found the theatre of Willowsleigh pretty, small, and inconvenient; he had rendered it by a few months' work, beautiful, spacious, and commodious, with an admirable auditorium and perfect acoustic effect. Now with little time and little effort he brought comrades of earlier days about him, and arranged for the production of his work on his own stage.

'It is when it helps us thus,' he said to Auriol, 'that money loses its coarseness, and becomes the nearest approach we have on earth to the blossoming of Aaron's rod, and the wings of Hermes' ankles.'

The wildest tales were circulated as to the fabulous sums which he had expended in mounting the work, and as to the beauty and extravagance with which this caprice was now to be carried out by him. No story was too absurd to be credited ; no conception too fantastic to be cited and believed. He had come back, as it were, from the grave, and he captured at a stroke the attention of Europe.

For himself all he thought of was one woman, and for her alone what he did was done.

He had that superb arrogance of genius which is no more vanity than the tread of the lion is the crawl of the cat ; he knew that none of those around her could give her what he could give ; he chose that she should know and feel and tremble before this power which was in him ; the whirlwind and the torrent of inspiration. He knew that his work was great ; that it was imperfect in many ways, but that it had the fire, the force, the sunrise beauties of a fresh and waking genius. It had poured out from his own life with all his passions incarnated in it; and rendered as he would render it, he knew that it would thrill through the sluggish pulses of the world like an electric current.

Passion has little place in the world, which is pale, and poor of spirit, and apathetic, and critical, and egotistic, and intent on formula and on minutiæ; yet it is a conqueror, a sorcerer, which even still scares the pallid cynics of the world with the wind of its rushing wings and the lightning flashes of its glorious eyes.

His play was founded on the tragic fate of Eleanora of Toledo at the hands of her husband Piero dei Medici; nothing could be less like in its terrible ferocity and naked passions to the impassive, polished, conventional routine of modern social life, and he believed that this divergence was so vast that it would suffice to prevent any possible parallel being instituted by his audience between the personages of the Renaissance and the men and women of his own generation and society.

Unconsciously he made the whole poem teem with allusions, emotions, reproaches, which were borrowed from his own feelings, and from their present position; whilst upon the figure of the Medicean voluptuary he cast all the ignominy, all the scorn, all the scathing irony, which it is possible for human language to convey. History does not tell us that Piero dei Medici killed his wife for any baser motive than the fury of a man paid in his own coin, and who, though faithless himself, forbids faithlessness unto himself. In the treatment of Syrlin's drama even this redeeming touch vanished, for he made a vehement desire for another woman the motive which instigated the tragic vengeance taken at Caffaggiolo. Under his treatment, when the Florentine prince hurried to the midnight murder he ceased to be, as history shows him to be, the just, though brutal, executioner of a faithless wife ; he became the murderer of an innocent and heroic woman because her life stood between him and the gratification of an erratic passion. Piero dei Medici filled the chief place on the canvas, and the character was portrayed with the minutest as with the boldest touches ; it stood out in its ignominy, and egotism, and meanness, and cruelty, instinct with meaning as Iago or as Cenci.

Syrlin was wholly unconscious himself of how completely his own hatred had coloured and vivified the portrait until it was a masterpiece of art, and also the indisputable likeness of a living man clothed in the costume of the Renaissance. In similar manner, and with no sense of his self-betrayal, he had put himself into the character of the lover, Bernardo Antinori, until his faults, his virtues, his ardour, his disdain, his love, his hatred, were all painted in it as the artist can paint his own form and features on a panel by aid of the mirror before him. Although deepened and heightened to the tone and the scale of the Renaissance tragedies, it was his and Avillion's own position, their own characters, their own motives, which were portrayed in the play. It was alive with a terrible force of life; not only that life which had been lived in the city palace and the mountain fortress, but that which with every moment throbbed and thrilled in his own veins. It is the kind of error that Marlowe or Musset would have made, had either been like him momentarily blinded and hypnotised by the pain and the rapture of a great and all-absorbing love.

Few men love thus now; but they had loved so in the days of Bernardo Antinori; and into the lifeless forms of these dead people he poured the galvanising breath of his own soul.

Unknown to himself he had poured out in his verse all the fury of his scorn for Avillion's amours, all the fires of his indignation for the slights and insults which were put upon Avillion's wife. He felt for her what she had never been within leagues of feeling for herself; he attributed to her sorrows which she had never even conceived in their faintest form; he imagined that she suffered as he, had he been a woman, would have suffered in her place; and all this he incarnated in his drama, in the wrongs and the temptations which he attributed to Eleanora of Toledo, and in the treachery and odium which he concentrated in the character of her lord.

In that blindness which comes with every strong passion, and in that naïveté which accompanies all intensity of genius, he never realised that others would pierce the slender disguises of his fictitious characters, that others would see the bare steel of his dagger shining through its embroidered scabbard. He never gave a thought to the danger of such an interpretation; and even if he had done, he would have considered that the exceeding difference of situation and of scene would suffice to prevent any association with the Medicean tragedy of any more modern types. Secure in that erroneous belief, he left free rein to the utterance of all which he felt and saw, and imagined that she felt and saw, and compensated to himself for the long silence and endurance imposed on him by allowing shape and substance, under the mask of dramatic illusion, to all the hatred and the devotion of his own heart.

He did not permit even Auriol to see the work in its entirety; his own self-consciousness made him sensitive over it as over the secrets of his own heart; alone, he read and re-read it, altered, improved, condensed, intensified it, adapted it to the necessities of representation as his experience enabled him to do, and realised that it was good with all that pleasure in the pride of creation which is so strong in the true artist and is so wholly unlike the vanity of the fool or the satisfaction of the mediocre.

To one judge only did he submit it lest his own feeling might mislead him; it was to his old master, the once great actor, Delessaint, freest, most delicate, and most unsparing of critics.

'*C'est une œuvre*,' said Delessaint when he had listened to it in silence from beginning to end, and Syrlin knew then that his imagination had not deceived, nor had his powers failed him.

Delessaint, who knew nothing of the personal hate and love which vibrated through the piece, was only sensible of its eloquence, its force, its admirably dramatic situations, its infinite variety of emotion, incident, and character.

'You have been a great interpreter of the creations of others,' he said to his favourite pupil, 'you will be a great creator yourself. I have always seen in you the soul of the poet. It is why you were often so galled and confined by the exigencies of the stage, often so insubordinate to usage and tradition. You made your career in triumph because genius has that wondrous facility which men understood entirely in the Renaissance, but which they now cannot understand or forgive. But the stage was only an *étape* for you on the march. You are made for greater things than even the interpretation of Racine and Molière. You are a part yourself. *Prends ton essor, mon fils. Ça te mènera loin.*'

Syrlin sighed as he heard. Even now, his wisdom whispered, it would be time still to turn away from this conventional existence which enervated, irritated, and destroyed him, time still to seek that virile and natural life where solitude and meditation would soothe his spirit, and danger and simplicity would brace his nerves and strengthen those powers of the mind which he felt within him, and which are the only true consolers of sorrow. It was still time to flee from all which he contemned, abhorred, despised: or it would have been time had not this fatal and overwhelming passion possessed him; had not his whole soul been set on avenging wrongs which he felt for her as she never felt them for herself, and had he not been blinded by his belief, that sooner or later she would turn to him for her solace and her vengeance.

He underrated the influence of habit and position; he over-estimated the forces of feeling and attraction; he judged her out of his own heart, and whilst he saw as weakness what she considered her strength, he failed to measure its power against himself.

Just such an error as led Chastelard to the scaffold, held him now in the world to which she belonged, a world which he despised and abhorred, and deemed of no more value than a handful of chaff, but which he could not bring himself to quit because it was that in which she lived and moved and had her being.

All he heard and saw of her husband's devotion to the Duchess de Charolois confirmed him in his erroneous impression, in his misleading hope, that offence and wounded dignity and just revenge would make her seek a champion, a redresser of her wrongs. He judged her by the fire of his own temper, by the romance of a poet's nature; he only vaguely and unwillingly saw that such a vindication of herself would only be still more offensive to her than the offence itself.

His blood was hot with the heat of Spain and Africa, his vision was coloured by the enthusiasms of a mind steeped in the poetries of all climes and ages. He felt all the forces of unspent, even of untried, powers fresh within him as virgin springs in the heart of a forest. He felt that his life was only in its commencement; that the laurels which he had gained were but as the crown of the neophyte, that he had the strength to compel success in fields wider and nobler than those in which he had hitherto been victor. But he knew also that all success, all creation, all triumph would be as nought to him beside the smile of a woman: a woman whose nature he knew could never answer his, whose soul was saturated with small things, whose heart was dried by the drying breath of the world, to whom love was a madness and genius a disease!

'Oh, accursed world! Why did I ever approach you?' he thought bitterly. 'Why did I ever give you my days and my nights, when the suns on the seas would have smiled on the one, and the moons on the mountains would have illumined the other? Why did I leave Nature for the crowd? When I was free to make my own fate, why did I not stay in the cities they call barbaric, in the peaceful monasteries, in the hills and the deserts with men whose hand is never given to a foe, and whose bread is never broken with dishonour? Why did I waste my youth and my heart in their wretched routine, in their gilded servitude, in their honeyed falsehood, in their sugared malignity, in their frothy vacuum? It was not my place, not my native air; my home should have been where the tents are set under the unsullied skies, where the horse is a friend, and the pulse and the waterspring are enough food and drink. I knew what life was; real life, simple, bold, free; I knew it—why did I ever forsake it?'

CHAPTER LIV

WHEN Avillion saw the card of invitation to Willowsleigh he laughed a little, good-humouredly.

'It will be interesting,' he said slowly. 'It is kind of him to give us a new thing.'

'You speak as if we should go,' said Freda involuntarily and imprudently.

'Of course we shall go,' said her husband pleasantly. 'Why not?'

She was annoyed, her eyes darkened, she looked away.

'Because he did not accept your—our—invitations,' she replied.

Avillion shrugged his shoulders.

'Oh, one must never take umbrage at the caprices of genius—or of lovers—both are like the people in the Gospel, they know not what they do.'

She was silent.

'We will both of us go,' he added in his most good-natured tone. 'It will be extremely interesting, exceedingly dramatic. Fancy a Musset acting a Fortunio, a Mounet-Sully writing a " Passeur " ! Have you any idea, by the way, of what the drama is about ? A *grande passion*, I suppose, and of course a hopeless one ? '

His wife felt for one fleeting moment that she understood the impulse which makes the ungoverned natures of the common people vent their irritation and their indignation in a blow.

She, polished, high bred, self-controlled, a great lady to the tips of her fingers, could only sit still, and smile a vague acquiescence, whilst she thrilled with unspoken anger under the gall and wormwood of insult.

'The devil take his impudence,' thought Avillion as he looked down on the card, which was worded a little as princes word those invitations which are commands. 'The devil take his impudence ! But at least *ça marche*. We shall probably get to a climax. It would be delightful. to send back his card and a horsewhip with it, but it would advance nothing. It would compromise me, not him.'

Avillion could be patient where his own malignities and interests were concerned, so that, meeting Syrlin in a club a day later, he saluted him graciously, and referred with amiable words to the intellectual and artistic pleasure to which he looked forward. Syrlin acknowledged his compliment briefly, and gave neither offence nor compliment in return.

A little later he met Avillion's wife at a great gathering in Belgrave Square.

'You will honour me at Willowsleigh?' he said to her coldly, and she replied as briefly :

'Lord Avillion is looking forward to it with much pleasure. All the world expects great enjoyment.'

She had avoided any possibility of being alone with him, even in such comparative isolation as is afforded by a conversation apart in some corridor, or boudoir, or conservatory of a great house when it is filled with people. A vague fear haunted her, and a faint sense of shame : the former lest he should compromise her before others, the latter because she knew that her neglect of him in his illness had been ungrateful and unworthy. Her consciousness of the ascendency he had over her, of the jealousy he could arouse in her, was a humiliation to her self-respect. The memory of the weakness which had overcome her beside the frozen reeds of the Swiftsure was with her at all times, and always she saw the gleam of ironical triumph in her husband's eyes, always she saw the soft slow pleasant smile with which he would note any such feebleness. That knowledge braced her into resistance. Never, never, never, let her suffer what she would, should Avillion have that joy for which he waited! Never should he have the luxury of looking at her with his courtly scorn, and murmuring 'How are the mighty fallen!'

Other women would have deceived their own souls and told themselves that this resolve was based on duty, honour, virtue, love of children, love of God; but she made none of these illusions to herself. She knew that the mainspring of her actions, the motive power of her conduct, was that sentiment which would never let her be humbled before her husband or her kindred.

It was that sentiment which Syrlin could but dimly comprehend, and which, had he understood it entirely, he would have utterly scorned. He could have had no sympathy with that perpetual consciousness which was ever with her, that the eyes of the world were for ever observing her, and that strength which she would have found to tear her very heartstrings asunder rather than afford food for laughter and censure to those whom she had so haughtily dominated for so long.

Avillion was ill pleased by the slowness with which the romance unfolded itself. It irritated and baffled him in every way to be unable to convict his wife of those sentiments and actions which he so desired to verify. Was it, he wondered impatiently, that the chilliness of her temperament really held in check her impetuous and imprudent adorer, or was it possible that both of them, by the ingenuity and subtlety which are lent to passion, were sufficiently adroit to deceive himself whom none could deceive? He regretted the temper which he had displayed about the Park riots, and was conscious that he had for once been ill-advised and childishly transparent. He should have been, he told himself, too much on his guard to have allowed any offence or coldness on his own part to interfere with his observation of Syrlin: such observation as is only to be obtained by intimacy with the person suspected. With all the grace and tact for which he was noted he set himself to undo this blunder, and to approach Syrlin anew with that admiration and artistic sympathy which he had honestly felt at the beginning of their acquaintance. But Syrlin was restive and reserved; and was neither to be allured nor blinded.

'You are so kind as to invite us ordinary mortals to your temple of the Muses; but why will you never honour our commonplace dwellings?' said Avillion in his blandest and sweetest tones one morning when they met each other by chance in Hyde Park.

Syrlin was silent; then he said abruptly:

'You have insulted me in the person of my friend.'

'Your friend? What friend? This is an enigma. Pray explain.'

'Auriol. I hear that your men of law intimate to him that he is unworthy the hand of your niece.'

Avillion stared, incredulous that he could hear aright.

'My dear sir,' he said vaguely, 'common-sense is not an insult. In these matters there is a received opinion current in society. No one goes against it. That is all.'

'What is your objection?'

'My objection? It is what my wife's is, what everybody's would be. It is not a matter open to discussion. I fully appreciat the accomplishments of your friend. Bu, you cannot seriously suppose that I should accept him as a suitor to Lady Ina.'

'It is because you do not that I have said you insult him and insult me in his person.'

'Oh dear no! There is no insult of any kind. There are received rules.'

'Is it his lack of fortune to which you object?'

'Oh dear no! It is—you must see for yourself what it is.'

'Would it be the same with myself were I Lady Ina's suitor?'

Avillion smiled faintly.

'Why will you put a painful hypothesis?'

Syrlin laughed a little coldly.

'The hypothesis is not painful to me. Your niece loves Auriol, and she shall be his wife sooner or later.'

'In that event her family—I regret to say it—but her family will certainly disown her. I do not believe such an event will occur. All girls have passing caprices. They are constantly enamoured of their music-masters.'

'Auriol is not a music-master.'

'Did I say that he was? I am so sorry,

so extremely sorry, to differ with you on any point, but upon this one I must. I am one of her guardians, and it is a question of duty. There are matters which are so obviously absurd that they should never be discussed. This is one of them.'

He raised his hat slightly with a pleasant smile, and sauntered on in an opposite direction.

Syrlin shook his head with an impatient gesture, like a horse which has been stung in the ear by a fly.

'We receive what we merit; Auriol was right,' he muttered. 'Why do we sing to them, play to them, dance to them; why do we let ourselves be the dupes of their fair phrases and their honeyed ways? We are only performing animals to them. It is our fault if we are kicked out when we presume on our popularity. Why do we antic in their drawing-rooms?'

On a sudden impulse he went to Avillion House, where he had never passed the gates since the day when Freda had refused to see him on her return from the Continent in the past autumn.

The servants recognised and admitted him; he was ushered into her presence, where she sat writing letters in her own room. It was the first time that they had been alone since the meeting by the river.

'Forgive me!' said Syrlin with hesitation, whilst his face grew very pale.

Her lips trembled slightly as she answered :

'You must forgive *me*. I did not ask for you in your illness. I—I—thought that you would understand why I did not.'

'I understood.'

A passing smile, melancholy and ironic, came for a moment on his lips.

'I did not come here to speak of myself,' he added. 'I want to speak to you of Auriol.'

She had not risen from her seat at her writing-table; she was sitting erect on a high straight-backed chair of gilded leather; her hand with its many rings lay on the table, the light from a window near fell upon her face and throat; there was something stately and regal in her attitude. He stood at the other end of the table, his eyelids lowered to hide the fires of adoration which glowed beneath them.

'I did not come to speak of myself,' he repeated. 'I want to speak to you of Auriol.'

'It is wholly useless.'

Her tone was chilling, but her heart thrilled with pleasure; it was only for his friend's sake that he had talked with Ina.

'Why useless?' he said earnestly. 'You speak of him as though he were a pariah. Your niece loves him, she has promised to be true to him; you can pain them, harass them, keep them apart for a time, but you will not be able to divide them for ever. Why torture them now? He is my well-beloved friend. I am rich as you know, I will give him half what I have and my house in Paris. They can lead simple, innocent, spiritual lives which will make the world the better for them. Why prevent or delay this because he is not, as I said once to you before, a bankrupt marquis, a drunken earl, a defaulter who is a duke's heir?'

Her fingers with their shining rings beat impatiently upon the table.

'All marquises are not bankrupt, all earls are not drunken. Your prejudices in one way are as great as are ours in another. It is wholly useless to speak of this matter. If you gave your friend a kingdom the thing would only be made more preposterous and remain equally impossible. Like mates best with like. It is an old homely English maxim, very wise. She must obey it.'

'And this wise axiom, Madame, has following it made or marred the happiness of your own life?'

The direct question embarrassed her. He spoke gently, still suppressing all the emotions at war within him, but its demand went home to her straight as a steel blade. Personalities are forbidden in social intercourse because their direct appeal is so hard to avoid or turn aside.

'I cannot allow such questions,' she said coldly. 'Neither you nor anyone has ever heard me complain of any circumstances of my life.'

'But we know that you bear, from dignity, patience, pride, generosity, what insults and hurts you with every day that dawns.'

'I think you exaggerate; and, at all events, I have never made you my confidant, in any way, on any matter.'

He was silent; to a frank nature, warm with unchecked feeling, and generous with chivalrous ardours, the artifice of an affected ignorance, the repulse of a simulated coldness, wound more deeply than the unkindest of rebukes.

'It is true,' he said at last humbly, ' you have not honoured me so far. But I see what all the world sees, and like the world I may be indignant at outrage to you.'

'Why will you use such *gros mots*? They are not of our day. I know of no outrage. If you mean to refer to the general conduct of Lord Avillion, I have nothing to complain of, for I have long given him entire liberty. And were it otherwise his caprices could be no concern of yours.'

The blood reddened his forehead.

'Give me only permission, and I will choke him dead like a noxious beast.'

She smiled, a little derisively.

'Poor Uther!' she said with a vague amusement. 'He is not made for dramatic treatment; of all men living he is the most modern. When will you remember that we are not upon the stage?'

'The passions on the stage were first copied from life, and I thought that you— you of all women—would not forgive insult? Is the parade of his adoration of Mme. de Charolois welcome to you?'

She bent and twisted in her fingers the quill pen she held.

'If it were not Mme. de Charolois, it would

be someone else less respectable; and it really does not matter to me. You will never understand. The one effort of our lives is to seem to see nothing which we do not wish to see, to avoid beyond everything else the comment, the laughter, or the pity of others. This seems to you very paltry, very false. To me it seems the natural conduct of all courageous and well-bred people. You and I look at nothing with the same eyes, nor with the same views. It is useless to argue. You view things like a cavalier of old Spain, or an Arab chief of the Sahara; I view them as a modern unit of a conventional world, whose gods are appearances and whose gospel is common-sense.'

'These are but words!'

'But words govern actions. You idealise me. You are wrong. I am the least idealic, I am perhaps the most selfish, of all women.'

He sighed heavily.

Circumstances, however contrary and stubborn, the bold may hope to change, but character the gods themselves cannot alter. He realised for a moment that he might break his heart for ever upon hers; the world would always be stronger with her than he.

'Let us talk of other things,' she said indifferently, but not with unkindness. 'Tell me of your play. What is its motive? What is its epoch?'

He did not seem to hear her: his eyes were gazing on her with burning adoration.

'That day by the river,' he murmured, 'I spoke to you too insolently, too violently; all that I felt carried me away, and I know that I justly incurred your anger. Every word was truth, every word was feeble to express the force of what I sought to tell; but I forgot that it would offend you, that it might sound like a menace and an insolence. I have repented it bitterly ever since. I will be whatever you dictate. I will ask nothing that you forbid. Only let me be your servant, your spaniel, your slave. I have been too rude and too arrogant to others; but to you I will be obedient as a dog. Only let me live in the light of your presence. Only let me think that your heart, in some measure, answers mine!'

She was silent some moments, whilst the sound of his quick and deep breathing was audible in the stillness.

'You like truth. I will give it you,' she said at last as she looked down on the writing-table before her, more agitated by his appeal than she would show. 'I would not have you pursue an illusive dream. I am not insensible to your devotion. I owe you a noble action ; you preserved me from insult, you probably saved my life. You are not—you cannot be —wholly indifferent to me, even though I may have seemed to you heartless and thankless. But I know myself. If you compromise me in any way—in the slightest way—I shall never pardon it, and I shall soon hate you. It may be selfish, it may be thankless, it may be mean ; but it is so. If you bring on me any comment from others, I shall see in you only an enemy ; I shall hate you. You have compared me to Mary Stuart ; I am like her in nothing else, but I should be like her•in this, I should never forgive the greatest love if it disobeyed me.'

'But if it obeyed you in the greatest as in the least?—if it only asked leave to give all and to claim nothing ? '

She hesitated ; she was moved to keen and warm emotions, such as had never agitated her in all her life before ; an unfamiliar weakness stole on her, sweet and insidious as the lulling charm left by opiates.

'I should be little worthy of it,' she said in an unsteady voice. ' What have you said yourself? " The world is too much with me."

It will be your rival and your enemy. I shall embitter your thoughts, waste your youth, consume your genius; for me you will fritter away your life in fretting impatience of all that is around me, in ill-recompensed submission to my caprices and my discontent. Leave me, leave me, leave me, whilst still it is time! Keep all these beautiful exalted feelings for some tenderer and kinder heart than mine. What can I give you in return? Nothing which will be worth one sigh of yours.'

'That is for me to judge. Such as my life is, it is yours. Yours only, yours always; yours to be passed in heaven or in hell as you may choose.'

He knelt before her on a sudden impulse as he spoke, his voice was sweet as music and tremulous with feeling, his eyes gazed up at her with imploring prayer more eloquent than all the language of the lips.

The womanhood in her could not wholly resist that sorcery of humility in one who never stooped or bent to man, yet from her would take the yoke of any slavery, however hard.

She turned her gaze on him with a fleeting and tender smile.

'You are unwise for yourself! What a burden you will lay on your freedom! But perhaps—if you always remember—if you always obey, I may—'

Her voice faltered, and her hand lay for a moment in his.

Why, she said in her heart, why should she live loverless all her life? And this man loved her as no other did, loved her supremely, indifferent to danger, submissive to unkindness, accepting all injury, seeing only on earth and in heaven but one law—her wishes and her will.

When he left her and passed out into the common light of day, he was as one drunk with the ecstasy of hope and of triumph. He had no sight for the multitude around him, no consciousness that men turned and stared at him, startled, they knew not why, by the rapt illumined dreaming joys revealed upon his face.

He knew well that he had given away his freedom and his future, that he would be no more the master of his fate; he knew that he would serve a sovereign who would place her foot on his bent neck; that he would give away to her all his best gifts—his youth, his pride, his genius, his liberty—and receive in return at best only a fleeting, secret, feverish happiness. He knew that she never would, that she never could, render back to him one thousandth part of that immense passion which he threw away upon her; it was not in her nature, or her knowledge, or her power. He knew that the world would be for ever a spectre to her sight, pale, cold, impalpable, but nearer to her than he. He knew the bondage, the tie, the sacrifice, which such vows as he had now sworn to her bring upon all men who are the loyal servants of their plighted word; he knew that he had made her mistress of his destiny, that he had given into her hands his will, his reason, and his soul, that never again would he be free to wander as he listed and shape his future as he chose.

He knew the world, and women and men, too well to be blind to the consequences of his own self-surrender. But his rapture outweighed and annihilated his wisdom. He loved, and was beloved: can a lover such as he weigh the measure of love's price?

That night he could not go into the world, not even to meet or follow her; he remained alone with his dreams and his desires in the moonlit silence of the dew-wet April woods.

These pale and level fields, these slowly budding glades, these dim grey gliding waters, which had seemed always to him so sad and sorrowful, now seemed lighted with a glory not of earth.

'She will be yours—yours—yours,' the river murmured, and the stars sang, the trembling moths whispered, and the wind-blown clouds cried aloud, the springtime going with him as he moved through the dusk with the breeze-borne pollen of the woodland blossoms fragrant on his hands.

'What are you doing there?' he said in anger as he saw the figure of Auriol awaiting him in the shadows; even the presence of his dearest friend seemed to him an unwelcome and insolent intrusion on his dreams.

'I could not sleep,' replied Auriol simply. 'I want to say something to you; it may irritate, offend, alienate you, but I must say it, or I shall never forgive myself for my own cowardice. I should have said it long ago.'

'Say on then,' replied Syrlin with impatience, his thoughts already straying away from the speaker.

'Is it wise, think you, to give that drama to the world?'

Syrlin stared at him.

'Your doubt comes late; on the eve of its representation!'

'It has come to me often earlier, but I feared to offend you. You are easily offended by any interference or apparent interference, and it is difficult to give my reasons without offence.'

'Keep them to yourself then. That is the wiser course!'

'But—if you will hear me—there are allusions, similarities, invectives in that play which will be apparent to your audience, too apparent. Is it well to show your heart, to strip your loves and hatreds naked like that to the world at large?'

Syrlin looked him coldly in the eyes. 'By what right do you conclude that there are either personal passions or actual situations in my work?'

Auriol hesitated. He knew nothing for certain; he only guessed what was suggested to him by his own observation and the words which he had heard from Syrlin in the incoherent utterances of fever.

'There are resemblances which no one can doubt,' he answered. 'The character of Piero dei Medici is the character of a man with whom you have already had differences, if not disputes.'

'The character of Piero dei Medici,' said Syrlin with violence, ' is that of every libertine and liar in our time as in his. Whoever recognises his own features in my portrait is welcome to do so. If he resent it, I shall be there to account to him.'

Auriol sighed. He had too little knowledge to have solid ground on which to base his objections; it was rather a presentiment which troubled and weighed on him than serious reasons such as he could hope would have weight with a wayward and self-willed nature like that of his friend.

Besides, the night was too near ; the preparations were too complete, the whole world of London had been invited there too publicly for the spectacle to be, at the last moment, abandoned. He did not venture to urge his views by naming those whose influence, as he conceived, had been so fatal to the destiny of his friend. He knew too little ; he feared to do more harm than good, and yet that instinct which is always keen in the artist's temperament made him apprehensive of a coming danger which was none the less oppressive to him because it took no definite shape.

Syrlin went past him without more words, and withdrew to his own chamber. The few sentences which had been already uttered had been enough to banish his dreamful peace and excite in him uneasy forebodings. What Auriol saw, would others see?

Reason, that calm, sad counsellor to which so few ever hearken, told him that his friend had spoken with more wisdom than he had been aware. Reason said to him now, whilst there was still time, to withdraw his tragedy from the world's hearing, to abandon under any pretence the representation of it, to take counsel with his own heart and with hers before giving its passionate verse to the chill critical comments of an indifferent society.

The glory of happiness which was within him was enough; what mattered it to him now to prove his strength in genius or art, or to reach the callous soul of his enemy by invective and by scorn? But he was a poet as well as a lover; he had in him the passion for his work as well as the passion for a woman. It was good in his sight, it would be great in the sight of the world. Fame was nothing to him, but the creator's joy in his creation was much. He longed for her to feel his power, to realise the sorcery at his command, to be witness of his supremacy and superiority over that world which had held her in its fetters for so long. There were passages in the drama which would avenge her on her husband for a decade of insult and infidelity. There were scenes in it wherein she would be forced to feel the empire and the excellence of those powers which she had so long regarded with indifference and disdain.

By the pure light of the dawning day he re-read those lines in which his own heart spoke, those soliloquies in which his hate and love thrilled through the disguise of fiction.

'She will understand, and he perhaps will wince under his triple shield of vanity and arrogance. No others will see anything,' he thought, reassured, as he murmured half aloud, in the first faint gleam of morning, those passages in which his own nerves had served as the chords of the lute.

For one moment more his reason spoke : it would be surest, it would be wisest, to invent any plea which might serve for the hour, and postpone the public representation of his work until her eyes had seen its text and her wish had decided its future.

But the impetuous passion of the artist was too strong in him to suffer that more prudent instinct to prevail. 'She loves me, and she will rejoice in my strength; he hates me, and he will learn that words can smite still deeper than the sword,' he thought, as the first rays of the sun fell across the pages of his manuscript. He looked up in the face of the day and smiled.

Life wore its loveliest smile to him.

CHAPTER LV

WHEN on the following morning Freda drove down through the pale sunshine and the flying dust of the London thoroughfares to attend once more the first Drawing Room of the year, she felt as though the whole world had changed and she with it, as though there were a new heart in her breast, a new soul in her body.

She seemed millions of miles away from this social atmosphere, which had been her only air so long; all the familiar sights and sounds seemed strange to her, and the noise of the wheels around her seemed to come from some far distance, as noise comes in a dream. She was not a woman who ever deceived herself. She knew that the future would be filled with those perils which she had always sworn to avoid. She knew that the man who is accepted as the woman's slave grows sooner or later into her master. She knew the imperious temper and the exacting passions of the lover who promised her eternal patience and endless submission. She knew the full truth of the old adage *Chateâu qui parle, femme qui écoute.*

She knew that one day or another, a day nearer or farther, but inevitable, she would see that triumph in her husband's eyes, she would see that smile of satisfied expectation on his lips, which she had vowed to herself a thousand times should never be allowed to come there.

She was herself no more. She felt as Mary Stuart may have felt when she had first stooped her royal head to hear the poet's vows.

It hurt her pride, it bent her strength ; and yet the whole fresh world of emotion which was opened by it before her, the new, warm sense of the full joys of living which it brought to her, were sweeter than was the bitterness of her own self-dethronement. She had loved no one in her life ; and she now loved him ; she could at last confess the supreme veracity of what she had deemed the baseless ecstasies of poets.

'But they have no place in such a life as mine,' she thought with a vague terror ; and, with a repentant self-knowledge, she thought also how little she was worth all that immense devotion, all that ideal worship!

The wheels rolled, the dust flew, the vulgar and prosaic noises of Piccadilly were around her, the news-boys bawled political news of Ireland and India, the cabmen's whips flicked the broken boughs of budding lilacs, the people hurried by, the weight of her tiara pressed on her head, the facets of the diamonds in her stomacher hurt her breast, the scent of the gardenias of her bouquet oppressed her.

'I am nothing that he thinks me!' she thought bitterly. 'I am only a woman of the world with one long day of small things, and a hard jewel where my heart ought to be?'

And yet she loved him; and a happiness such as she had never dreamed of was awake within her, and for a fleeting moment she felt that she would take off her diamonds, and lay down her tiara, and turn her back upon this foolish, fretful, cumbersome, conventional world, and go away into some fair strange land where she could be alone with him and nature.

The voice of Avillion called her back to fact and to himself.

'You are looking very well to-day, my lady,' he said pleasantly. 'Would you mind my putting this window up? There is a sharp tinge in the wind and my throat is troublesome. And would you kindly hold those gardenias a little further away? I am like the virgin in "Le Rêve"; the odour of voluptuous flowers is too much for my nerves.'

CHAPTER LVI

THE same evening was the date of the representation of 'Le Glaive.'

Her courage failed her when the day arrived, and she was sorely tempted to make excuse for her absence on one of those vague unchallengeable pleas of health which are always weapons at the hand of every woman. But Avillion, with a persistency which he had never displayed on any similar occasion, so minutely inquired into her reasons and put such urgency into his wishes that she should appear at Willowsleigh, that she yielded and agreed to go there.

'It would be an *affaire manquée* without you,' said her husband in a tone of amiable innocent banter. 'Chastelard would be quite capable of not appearing at all if his Queen put such an affront as her absence upon him. Besides, I am sure it will be interesting, extremely interesting ; why should you be so anxious to miss the great dramatic event of the year?'

'It is a long way off, and I am not perfectly well.'

'No?'

Avillion looked at her with a smile, that smile which she dreaded.

'You were looking remarkably well at the Drawing Room. You look very well to-day; you have recovered your colour. Pallor does not become you. Oh, you must certainly come down to-night. I quite understand, the whole thing is given for you. It interests me extremely. He serves up his own heart at the banquet as the knight did the falcon, as the gods did the boy Itys. Nothing can be more interesting.'

He laughed, a low pleasant laugh, such as made it impossible to take his bantering words with any serious offence, though her blood thrilled with anger and her face flushed as she heard.

'If you have such an opinion,' she said curtly, 'I wonder you honour the entertainment.'

'Why?' said Avillion with an innocent stare. 'The eccentricities of genius are always condoned; and a poet has full right to sacrifice anything to the Muses, his own soul if he pleases. I am only so glad that he recovered from that fever, for it would have been such an affecting remembrance to both of ushad he died of the exposure on our Yorkshire moors.'

He sauntered towards the door as he spoke; then turned back and said in the same careless and amiable tone:

'By the way, Claire de Charolois has no card; he does not know her; and she wishes to go. Will you fill in a blank one? I am sure he has given you heaps of blank ones.'

'You can ask him for one yourself.'

'There is no time. I did not know till last night late that she cared about it. I am sure he has put dozens at your disposition. Give me one.'

She knew very well that it was only said to irritate her, to give her fully to understand the conditions on which his amiability and acquiescence were to be secured; that it was one of many other equivalents and humiliations which she would have to accept and to endure in days to come; that it was, in a word, a slight thing, but a compendium of that mutual conjugal pact which would be henceforth obligatory upon her, and which had always seemed to her in others so contemptible and so disgraceful.

Avillion stood a moment waiting, not annoyed, not impatient, slightly amused, conscious of his own mastery.

An intensity of hatred passed through her and dwelt sombrely in her eyes for a moment, as she went to her writing-table, the same at which Syrlin had stood forty-eight hours before, and opening one of the drawers took one of the invitation cards out of it and wrote across the blank left for the purpose the name of the Duchess de Charolois. She handed it to her husband in silence.

'So many thanks,' he murmured as he took it with a gracious inclination before her. 'By-the-bye, what is the story of "Le Glaive?" What is its motive? There are many versions about the town. Of course you have read the manuscript or had it read to you?'

'I have no idea whatever of its plot,' she replied truthfully. 'I have not heard or seen a line of it. But I believe it is founded on some romance of Italian history.'

'Ah, so wise!' said Avillion putting his card into his breast pocket. 'Nowadays we do not lend ourselves to dramatic treatment. There are the same passions, but they are conventionally treated; just as there is the same anatomy in a nude figure of Michael Angelo's as there is under a suit of nineteenth-century clothes; but what a difference in appearance! We cling to our clothes—to our conventional treatment—with all the force there is in us. They are so useful, and we think them even becoming. So many thanks. *Au revoir.*'

He went away with his slow indolent gait, his graceful ease, his agreeable smile, and his wife looked after him with that hatred in her gaze which might, had he turned and seen it, have brought home to him the truth that 'conventional treatment' may even in .the close of the nineteenth century be sometimes set at naught. She understood very well; the card was but a pretence, Claire de Charolois must have had her card already; it was but an item on which it pleased him to insist in that long list of concessions which he would henceforth make her sign. There is a forcible expression in French which has no equivalent in English: *avaler des couleuvres.* She felt as though she had swallowed many, and her proud nostrils quivered less with pain than with disgust and hatred.

When the evening came she dressed to go

to Willowsleigh like all the world: she knew that her absence would awaken remark and confusion. As she descended the staircase, to her surprise, Avillion joined her.

'Allow me to go down with you,' he said pleasantly. 'Let us honour this memorable occasion by full etiquette. You have no one with you? Not even Ina?'

'Can we take Ina where Auriol is? And where his music will be given?'

'Ah, no, true: I always forget these salad loves,' he replied good-humouredly, as he went down the stairs by her side.

Throughout the long drive, made longer by the great number of carriages following the same route, he was agreeable, amusing, exquisitely polite: the visible trouble and constraint of his wife pleased him. It would be strange, he thought, if during the course of this momentous evening she, or Syrlin, did not betray themselves or each other to his vigilant and penetrating eyes.

The whole of society was driving towards Willowsleigh in the April night, which was mild and damp but rainless, with the scents of spring floating through the shadows under the stars, and lending freshness and sweetness even to the hackneyed and commonplace high road. The park and gardens were illuminated; the house was outlined with stars of light; the terraces were lit in the old Florentine fashion, pages in Renaissance costume stood down the stairs with flaming torches: within doors the stately graces of a Florentine pageant had been copied as closely as possible. The great people as they arrived were charmed and amazed.

'He knows how to do the thing,' murmured Avillion approvingly. 'If the intellectual be as good as the decorative part of this affair we shall enjoy our evening.'

The easy amiability of the tone struck terror into his wife's heart as she heard; whenever he was thus contented, thus willing to praise, he had always some drift of selfish purpose, some expectation of selfish success. She entered the theatre with a sick sense of alarm outweighing for the first time her natural imperious spirit.

The house was crowded, the assemblage the choicest which Europe could offer; royal people occupied the armchairs in the centre of the auditorium, banks and aisles of flowers filled the air with perfume. The curtain was a beautifully painted view of the Florence of the Sei Cento; banners bearing the arms of the Italy and the Spain of the Renaissance drooped above it. The orchestra was unseen. In its place was a parterre of blossoming roses. On the whole was shed a veiled and softened light. Pages passed noiselessly between the lines of chairs, offering to each lady a bouquet of lilies of the valley and a copy of the list of names of characters and players illuminated on vellum by a clever artist.

She looked down on hers, and saw but one name which, for her, obliterated all the others.

Bernardo Antinori :—Syrlin.

The once small and ordinary playhouse of Willowsleigh had, under his alterations and additions, become a theatre fit for a sovereign, and he had interested himself in all its details, dreaming always of her presence in it and of the possible pleasure which she might take in its entertainments and successes.

When the curtain drew up, and the drama began, it was found admirable in its beauty of scene, in its splendour of decoration, in its perfection of impersonation. The most brilliant of his comrades of France had gladly obeyed his invitation to take part in an event of such extreme interest, dramatic and poetic.

The greatest names of the Français and Odéon were upon the list of his players, and all that exquisite intuition, perfect habitude, and admirable comprehension can do for the representation of any dramatic work were done by them for his.

Nothing that money or taste or art could do to enhance the beauty and illusion of the scene had been spared ; and the first scenic artists of the time had created for him the beautiful city of the Medici, and the austere stateliness of the Villa of Caffaggiolo, the carnival pageantries and masques, the assembling of the steel-clad condottieri, the magnificent Medicean court, the public square before the Communal Palace, the tapestry-hung and frescoed chamber where Eleanora of Toledo met her death at her lord's hands.

It was a year of the Renaissance revived in all its splendour, colour, movement, tragedy, and glory ; and across the superb picture moved, as on an illuminated background, the figures of the cruel and polished voluptuary, of the lonely and lovely Spanish woman, of the lover who was at once a soldier and a poet.

As the dazzling beauty of the scenes succeeded each other in harmonious sequence, the audience, sated, critical, hard to rouse and to please though it was, was charmed into a breathless interest and delight, whilst a subtle sense of coming woe, of destined danger, was felt through all the festive gaiety, the poetic courtship, the revelry, the splendour, the music, and the wit.

In no moments of his greatest triumphs had Syrlin been more supremely master of the hearts of his audience, had more entirely moved them to all the gamut of emotion at his will. His personal beauty was set forth in its utmost perfection in the costume of the Florentine youth, his dark hair cut straight across his brows, and his tall and slender form clothed in the blue and gold of the Antinori, with their badge embroidered on his breast and arm. His own verse rang from his lips, now sonorous and defiant as a silver clarion, now sweet as the south wind in summer, now tremulous with sighs which brought tears to the eyes of every woman there.

To be loved thus, who would not dare the fate of Eleanora? was the unspoken thought of more than one who hung upon his accents.

The first act, and the second, passed in uninterrupted triumph, greeted by an ecstasy of applause in which the coldest and most hypercritical of audiences was startled into such rapture and such homage as, when the century was young, once greeted Talma.

When the curtain fell upon the close of the second act many of his guests drew a deep breath and looked in each other's faces, startled and amazed, as though they had been visitors to some enchanted land, wafted thither by a magician's sorcery, and were now rudely awakened to find themselves once more on earth. Avillion's countenance alone was impassive; and on his brows there was a cloud; some of the barbed shafts of the innuendoes and rebukes had already pierced the triple armour of his vanity and pride.

'This mime has dared to summon me to lesson me!' he thought in rising wrath.

The face of his wife was very pale; the dread which had been in her, faint and slight, had deepened with each syllable she heard as the characters and the situations of the play unfolded themselves. She felt as those felt of old who heard the voice of Apollo at Delphi, knowing that an inexorable fate would speak in it, and shrinking from its dread decree. Entranced at first, like all others, by the beauty of the scene and the eloquence of the verse, she had listened with gradually growing apprehension and alarm as little by little the story was revealed and the personages delineated.

'Is he mad?' she thought. 'Was inspiration insanity as the Greeks believed? Could he wittingly satirise and censure such a man as Avillion before the whole gathered society of his world?'

She felt like one paralysed, who watches a blow descending—descending—descending—and is powerless to move, or speak, or stay the fatality of its stroke.

She had to conceal all she felt, to sit still in her chair between a duke and an ambassador, to murmur her assent to the eulogy, to beat polite applause with the sticks of her fan on the palm of her hand, to feel or to imagine that all eyes in the crowded auditorium were fastened upon her, and to wear all the while a carefully composed expression which should denote strong impersonal artistic interest and hide all personal feelings. Once she glanced to where her husband sat on the other side of the theatre; she saw by the line between his eyebrows, by the hauteur upon his features, that he saw what she saw; his eyes met hers for an instant, and they were keen as steel.

'You have known that this was to be!' that

swift hard accusing glance said to her in language unread by any other.

The unseen orchestra was making the delicate and profound music of Auriol steal like an enchanted flute from a bower of palms; the whole audience was wrapt in a mute and delicate delight; no one spoke above a whisper, the most careless, the most cultured, the least prone to emotion or to admiration, were moved to a hushed and eager expectation; the dazzling scene swam before her eyes, the weird electric lights quivered before her sight, all her awakened heart was filled with the beauty and the genius of the man she loved; and yet a wave of furious rage passed through· her against him.

Through him, and through his mad imprudence, her name would be the fable of the whole town on the morrow!

With thickly beating pulses, and a sound like rushing water in her ears, she awaited the closing act of the drama. Perhaps, she thought, after all, what she saw and heard in it no one else would perceive; perhaps, she told herself, it was merely because her consciousness made her a coward that she imagined resemblances which only existed in her imagination. But that glance from her husband had told her that he at least saw what she saw, heard what she heard, and was awaiting the development of the action with the amazed fury of a man who had never suffered from any living being censure or rebuke. Outwardly he was calm, indifferent, attentive; he bent his graceful head to Mme. de Charolois, beside whom he sat, and applauded with the rest; but his wife knew the meaning of that line between his brows, knew the meaning of the one look which he had given to her. The insult which he was passively receiving was the most offensive which could have been offered, for it was an insult which, whilst it was inflicted in public, it was yet impossible in public to resent.

The music filled the air with cadences in which the destinies of the doomed lovers seemed foreshadowed; the odours of the exotic flowers seemed to have poison in their sweetness; in the murmuring voices around her she fancied that she detected phrases of ridicule, of sarcasm, of wonder; in all the radiant, courtly, perfumed atmosphere there seemed to her awakened apprehensions only mockery, menace, obloquy.

It was her own world which was around her, the world of her relatives, her friends, her associates; if they comprehended the undercurrent of meaning with which every word of the drama seemed charged to herself, what would the morrow bring? She was avenged by it on her lord, indeed; but like Eleanora of Toledo he would make her pay for her vengeance with her life. Courage had never failed her in her whole existence before; but now it seemed fainting and dying in her; passion and tragedy had been alien to her, abhorrent to her, unknown to the world in which she dwelt, and now they were loosed upon her like sleuth-hounds beyond all escape.

As her glance rapidly and secretly swept over the countenances around her she thought she saw on every face a smile, she thought she heard in every murmur a word of derision. Could all the joys and all the genius on earth compensate to her for being made for one moment thus the target of a social jest?

If he had only told her, prepared her, submitted his work to her judgment, she would have forbidden its production. Oh, fool that she had been, not to foresee and avert the peril! Had not the song of the gardens of Holyrood been warning enough of the rashness, and ignorance, and fatal candour of his love for her?

The third act began.

The curtain rose upon an evening scene, and the lovely moonlight of a Florentine night shone upon the terraces and towers and shining river of the city.

Bernardo Antinori stood in the shadow of the Hospice of the Knights of Malta, and spoke with a friend of Piero dei Medici, the abhorred and faithless lord of the woman whom he himself worshipped.

The white rays from the moon shone on his features, a noble scorn, a vehement hate, the scorn of a knight for a caitiff, the hate of a loyal soul for a treacherous nature, blazed in his eyes, and rang from his lips, as Syrlin came down the centre of the stage and stood alone, looking upon his drawn sword, and speaking to his comrade behind him, of the man he loathed, in verse which rang through the theatre like a challenge to mortal combat.

> Impur et impudique, il cherche ses amours
> Dans la fange du brutal et vénal concours
> Des beautés se livrant à l'amant le plus riche
> Partout où Volupté languit et se niche,
> Sur le sein satiné d'une reine du monde
> Ou les flancs inféconds d'une bacchante immonde ;
> Mais son épouse doit rester aux fonds des bois,
> Soumise à ses vouloirs et subissant ses lois.

Il insulte son trône, il outrage sa cour,
Où vient se succédant la maîtresse du jour,
S'incliner sur sa main, mais son orgueil flétrir,
Tandis que souriante elle doit tout subir
Sans se permettre un mot, sans jamais se trahir,
Par sa fierté dressée, et forcée de mentir,
Car noblesse oblige à la femme ! Quant a lui,
Il est duc, il est prince, il est pair—grand Dieu, oui !
C'est tout ce qu'on demande à des gens de sa sorte.
C'est un cuistre, une brute, un lâche, mais qu'importe ?
Le monde observe-t-il un blason de si près ?
De loin voit-on la boue au pied du fier cyprès ?

. . . . . .

The scathing lines left his lips with a terrible meaning, a withering scorn, and forgetful of the part he played, of the mask of fiction which alone made such an utterance possible, he approached nearer to the footlights and looked point blank at Avillion where he sat beside Claire de Charolois.

There was an instant's silence in which all the spectators present drew their breath with oppression, dreading what was next to come : no one there present failed to understand the intention and the invective ; and the woman whom he had thought to honour and to avenge felt in that moment that she could have killed him with her own hands.

The words rang out, clear, scathing,

terrible; his glance flashed to where his enemy sat, and challenged him like a spoken defiance.

Then the action of the work continued without pause; a crowd of citizens, soldiers, courtiers, filled the stage; the dialogue, interrupted for an instant, was resumed, carrying on the development of the story, and leading the way by subtle and artistic degrees towards the catastrophe of its close.

But the insult had been given and had been received, and all the London world had seen and heard and understood its meaning.

Avillion, for an instant, had grown livid with rage and made an involuntary movement as if to rise; the next moment, self-command and conventional habit resumed their power; he remained in his place, giving no other sign, attentively following, or so it seemed, every incident and every phrase of each succeeding scene.

His wife, very pale, but mistress of herself, appeared to do no less, although in truth she was conscious of nothing except the trumpet sound of those terrible verses which echoed in endless reverberation on her ear, and the magnetic force of those lustrous eyes which ever and again, as Syrlin came and went upon the stage, sought hers with passionate appeal.

The drama, henceforth closely following history, passed on to its climax where Piero dei Medici, kneeling first to ask forgiveness of heaven for his act, slew his wife with his own hand in the solitude of Caffaggiolo, whilst in the city below, her lover perished upon the scaffold.

The whole work was great: Greek in its visible vengeance of the gods and pitiless approach of destiny; Italian in its subtlety, its ardour, its cruelty; Renaissance in its gorgeousness and movement; modern in its melancholy, in its psychology, in its analysis of motive and hereditary taint. Its influence was immense, its beauty undoubted, its genius supreme; it was a triumph of the senses, of the arts, of the intellect, of all the various forces which must combine in one perfect whole to produce a work of genius. The coldest and most sated of audiences was moved by it to an ecstasy of admiration, to an intensity of emotion, whilst the sense of personal meaning, the consciousness of impending peril, with which it was accompanied, heightened the force of its sway over the minds of all who witnessed and who heard it.

No one looked openly at Avillion: all

thought of him and glanced furtively to where he sat, impassive, and apparently unmoved, leaning back in his armchair whilst the applause of the audience recalled Syrlin again and again and again before the curtain to receive the meed of his double triumph as actor and as poet, and the women in the ardour of their emotion rose from their seats and threw to him the bouquets from their hands and the flowers from their breasts.

But when the auditorium began to empty and the spectators passed out to the adjacent gallery where the supper-tables were spread, Avillion rose, and with a murmured word in the ear of Claire de Charolois, passed rapidly round to the wings, and forced his way through the press of the actors and supernumeraries to the dressing-chamber where Syrlin was rapidly changing his Florentine costume for ordinary evening clothes.

Avillion went straight up to him and struck him in the face with his glove.

'You will meet me at St. Germains the day after to-morrow,' he said briefly. 'A gentleman need not meet a comedian and a bastard, but I will do you that honour.'

Syrlin, who was standing stripped to his shirt, knocked him down.

'Get me fresh linen,' he said with a superb insolence to his servant. 'This is soiled, for it has touched him!'

Whilst other men surrounded Avillion, who was for the moment stunned, he dressed rapidly and hurried to join his guests and do the honours of his house to the royal personages who were present.

His blood ran like flame in his veins. He was scarcely conscious of what he did or said, though he bore himself with outward composure. His pulses thrilled with delight at having at last reached his foe. His pride burned with rage at the insult he had received, and with triumph at the insult which he had given, and his eyes anxiously sought for the face of the woman he loved, whilst he thought, 'Is she glad, is she angered, does she think it well done, will she rejoice that I have avenged her?'

Without her praise what worth would be the homage of all Europe? Unless she were content, what joy would there be in either victory or vengeance?

Avillion had immediately left the house, and no one knew anything of the scene which had taken place in the dressing-room. People noticed his withdrawal from the party as a singular violation of etiquette, since the royal persons had remained to supper; but no one asked indiscreet questions, and everyone understood the offence which the soliloquy in the opening of the third act and many other passages in the play must have caused to him. The knowledge of that unexplained insult, that veiled outrage, and their ignorance of how it would be accepted or avenged, lent to the brilliancy of the evening for those present that charm which lies in mystery and danger. As at the banquets and pageants of the Medicean time, the dagger and the axe seemed suspended by a thread above the revellers.

His wife, noting his absence, invented for him an excuse of sudden indisposition to the princes and princesses. She knew nothing herself of the blow which had been given and returned, but she imagined that some great quarrel must have taken place, some terrible chastisement been given or received, and her lips were white as they smiled and spoke the polished babble of society.

A deadly and bitter anger, great as her lord's, consumed her. She had forgotten all except the injury received; she sat at the supper-table crushing her wrath into her own breast, burning for the time when she could pour it out in words. It seemed to her as if the entire night waned away, and yet she was compelled to remain there; seated at the royal table to which she had been invited, forced to smile, to converse, to laugh, to listen, to keep up that comedy of society which she had played so long, and which was now to her so intolerable a torture.

She never looked at Syrlin once. He could not tell what she felt, what she thought, what she wished. An agony of anxiety tortured him; an agony of apprehension began to chill the exaltation and exultation in him.

The royal persons remained hour after hour, amused, fascinated, unwilling to leave an entertainment which had so novel a charm for them, and in which they, like others, vaguely suspected the storm on the horizon, the death in the cup.

When they at last took their departure there was the usual stir and change of place which follows on the withdrawal of royalty from any entertainment. There were dancing in the ball-room, a concert in the music-gallery, card-tables set in the long chamber hung with the Gobelins. No one was willing to leave a scene so brilliant, an evening which everyone foresaw would be so memorable.

In the general animation Syrlin ventured to approach her; his gaze was suppliant, his attitude was timid. All through the supper he had watched her with a beating heart, a quickening apprehension; a ghastly fear began to assail him that he had offended and alienated her.

'Might I have the honour to take you to the music-room?' he murmured as he bent to her. 'There is a new cantata of Saint-Saëns' now beginning there.'

He paused, chilled to the bone by the indefinable expression of her eyes as they glanced at him.

'With pleasure,' she said, as she rose and accompanied him.

But midway to the concert-chamber, from which the sounds of a trio of violins came sweetly, she withdrew the touch which she had laid upon his arm.

'I have to speak to you. Come out into the air,' she said, as she moved towards a bay-window which opened on one of the garden terraces.

She pushed the glass door open, and walked out on to the terrace, lighted like the gardens in the old Florentine manner, by multitudes of little lamps which shone like fireflies amongst the foliage.

'You will take cold; the dawn is chilly,' he murmured anxiously, whilst his eyes gazed down on her with longing and suppliant passion.

She took no notice of his words, but went a few paces out into the chilly gloom; the night was fair but cold, above the woods there was the gleam of day.

Once out of the sight and hearing of others, like a lioness, she turned upon him, her white shoulders gleaming in the lamplight, her diamonds glittering upon her head and breast and arms.

'How dare you?' she said between her clenched teeth. 'How dare you? How dare you?—'

She could for the moment find no other words.

He thought that she asked him how had he dared to strike her lord.

'He struck me; I struck him,' he answered sullenly. 'He has received his deserts—for once.'

'You struck him—when?'

He then saw that she knew nothing of the scene which had taken place in the dressing-room. But it was too late to retract the admission, or to avoid its consequence.

'Behind the scenes, in my own cabinet,' he muttered. 'He insulted me first. He received what he merited.'

'If he struck you he did well,' she said bitterly. 'It is the first act of his life that I admire and respect. How dared you to resent it? You have no title to resent.'

'Why?'

'Why? Can you ask me why? Because you have violated the first principles of hospitality and good faith. You have invited a guest to outrage him before his friends. You have taken advantage of his compliment to you to fling an insult in his face. Do you know anything of honour? What would the Arabs you admire say to you? Their worst foe is sacred when he crosses their threshold. But you—you asked us here to humiliate us before all the world, to make our name a fable in men's mouths. What are my lord's follies or faults to you? Who bade you rebuke them? Who will ever believe that I was ignorant of what you meditated? Who will ever credit that I had not read your play and did not bring my husband and Mme. de Charolois here to be subject to your outrages? Who will ever believe that I was not your accomplice and your instigator?'

The words scourged him like whips. He stood stunned and defenceless before her. The whole extent of his offence flashed before him in a sudden revelation.

She, cruel as women almost always are cruel when the mastery is theirs, stood under the silvery lights of the lamps, with her incomparable beauty shining in its perfection before his eyes, her nostrils dilating, her bosom heaving, in the intensity of a wrath for which all language seemed too poor.

'Only two days ago,' she said; 'only two days ago, I warned you that if you ever compromised me in the slightest way I should hate you, and you had not the common candour, the common honesty, to tell me then that you meant to disgrace me before all my world! I knew you were rash, I knew you were blind, I knew you were often mad; but how could I conceive such treachery, such conspiracy, such infamy as this? If my lord struck you he did well; woman though I am I could find it in me to strike you myself!'

A quiver passed over him as she spoke; he saw that never—never—never whilst her life should last, would he have credence or forgiveness from her.

'I did not know,' he stammered timidly, 'I did not think. I thought he would understand,—that no one else would know—he has deserved worse things than this.'

'What he deserves, what he does not deserve, what is either to you? Did ever I bid you be my redresser or my champion?'

'No. But—'

'But your own unbridled fancy, your own intemperate imagination, led you into a thousand beliefs which had no foundation in any fact on earth! You have genius no doubt, but you have the madness of genius, and its perfidy. You have made me conspicuous, odiously conspicuous, ever since the first night I saw you. I would far sooner the mob had stoned me to death than have lived for the stare and the sneer of my world to night.'

A low cry broke from him like the cry of some noble animal slain by the hand it adores.

'I will try to undo what I have done,' he said inarticulately. 'But it was done in ignorance. Forgive me, for—for—I love you so well!'

She looked at him with cruel pitiless eyes of hatred.

'I will never forgive you,' she said with slow and bitter deliberation. 'I will never forgive you. And you can undo nothing you have done.'

All the arrogance and haughty temper which had been in her nature from her birth, and which education and position had restrained from expression, broke out into vehement utterance now, when to the anger roused in her was joined the sense that she felt in her, for the man whom she tortured, the passion which she had so long derided and denied.

She turned away to approach the house.

'Stop, for God's sake, and hear me!', he cried piteously. 'I never thought of any publicity; I believed that he might know, that you might see, some truth in my play : but that was all. I fancied that you would approve.'

'Approve? I?'

She looked over her shoulder at him, the blue of her eyes flashing with cruelty and scorn.

'Approve! That my husband should be insulted before all his family and friends? That a woman who is my acknowledged rival should think that I could stoop so low as to plot or plan with you an affront to her?

Sur le sein satiné d'une reine du monde!

Who could doubt the line was meant for her? Who could ever be brought to believe that I did not agree to, rejoice in, combine with you, all these infamies? Do you know nothing of the common rules of honour, of society, of life? You involve me in what must look to everyone a disgraceful conspiracy, and you do not seem even to comprehend the evil which you have done! Cannot you imagine a little what will be said in every house this morning? The princes themselves —all—everyone—what must they think of me? You affect loyalty and adoration, you promise obedience and consideration, and the way you keep your vows is to degrade me in the esteem of all my world? I will never pardon you; I will never receive you; I will never speak to you again. I warned you that I should loathe you if you drew any slander on my name. I blush to remember that I was weak and infirm of purpose enough to believe for a single hour that I loved you.'

He put out his hands in a gesture of supplication.

'For pity's sake spare me! I did not know—'

'You did not know! You have lived on

the stage and you think that a gentlewoman is to be courted like a strolling player's quean! I am punished, justly punished. I have stooped to you; and you have abased me before all the town. Your presence is odious, your worship is degradation. You have acted like a coward and a traitor. I hate you, I hate you, I hate you! I loathe to think that, in an hour of weakness, I was base enough to listen to your vows!'

Her whole form dilated with the intensity of her passion. She was indifferent how she hurt, how she stung, how she maddened him; he was nothing to her in that moment but a slave to be scourged and hounded from her presence.

She again turned away to enter the house; but he caught the folds of her train in his hands.

'Stop, for God's sake, stop!'

She shook him off and passed onward without a relenting glance or a gentler word.

He stood dumb and motionless from the intensity of his anguish, great tears gathered slowly in his eyes and fell one by one down his cheeks.

He watched her enter the house and pass from sight; the white clearness of daybreak was growing broader and brighter above the river, but on him the darkness of an eternal night had fallen.

He stood awhile where she had left him, then went slowly and with uncertain feet, like a blind man, down the steps of his terrace, and into the deep cool shadows of the blossoming woods.

CHAPTER LVII

EARLY in the forenoon Avillion received a letter.

A quarter of an hour after the receipt of it, he sent word to know if his wife would accord him ten minutes' audience. She had not been to her bed; she had been sleepless, feverish, unnerved; the day which she had seen dawn on the terrace of Willowsleigh could bring her no peace; as yet the intensity of her wrath was undiminished, unsubdued; the bitterness of the offence was unquenchable; she loathed the sight of the morning; all over the town she knew that people were talking of her, some with pity, some with ridicule, some with scorn. The arrogance of her soul writhed within her as she thought of all the manifold aspects in which her friends or foes would view the scandal of the past night, all, whether in amity or enmity, being agreed to blame, to sneer, to deride, to jest, to rejoice that on the white ermine of her robes there was a stain at last!

There was no repentance in her for the ferocity and the cruelty of her own words. In memory they only seemed to her too sparing, too few, too meagre. She clenched her hands when she recalled them in their impotence. She understood now how Mary Stuart had bidden the axe fall.

When she received the message of her lord she braced herself to pass through a cruel scene.

She knew his nature; she knew that no subtlety, ingenuity, and brutality of vengeance on herself would content him; and she knew also that it would be utterly hopeless ever to force him to believe in her complete innocence of any share or any foreknowledge of the insult which he had endured. She looked for no mercy at his hands. Though he could prove no guilt upon her, he would drive her from her place if fraud or force could do it.

Standing on the hearth of her morning-room she awaited his entrance; she was cold, austere, pale, prepared to be assailed by his invective and abuse, indifferent to whatever chastisement he might inflict, ready once for all to tell him all she knew of his hidden life. When he was ushered in to her, he stood a moment hesitating and troubled; shaken for once out of his bland and cynical calm.

He held an open letter in his hand, and he hesitated a moment before he spoke; then in a harsh, hushed voice he said to her:

'Madam, your lover shot himself this morning by a boat-house in his woods where arms were kept! He has worsted me to the last. One cannot make a dead man a co-respondent. But I am not his dupe or yours.'

Then he gave her the letter which he held; a letter written to him briefly, and in haste.

'My Lord,—I will not wait to receive my death from you; I have done wrong, and I expiate it. Your wife has never loved me, and she knew nothing of the purport of my play. I have long left all that I possess to my friend, Auriol; give him the hand of the young girl whom he loves. It is the only favour I ask of Lady Avillion.'

The letter was signed 'Syrlin.'

She read it from the first line to the last, calmly, steadily, without any sign of feeling; then swaying to and fro for a moment, she fell forward senseless on her face.

Avillion stood awhile looking down on her in her insensibility with a strange look upon his countenance; half exultation and half disappointment, half triumph and half defeat.

Then he stooped and took the paper out of her clenched hand, for servants are curious, and leaving the room with his indolent, unhurried step, said to the footmen in the antechamber:

'Her ladyship is not quite well. Send her women to her.'

Then he sauntered gently through the corridors to his own apartments.

'He has outwitted me to the last, curse him!' he murmured, half aloud. 'There is no plea for divorce to be found in these lines. What a fool to die for *her*! Oh, heavens, what a fool!'

L'ENVOI

CONSUELO LAURENCE was alone in her drawing-room in Wilton Street.

It was twilight, and when the servant had entered to light up the rooms she had told him to go away for half an hour. She had given herself the luxury of being denied to all visitors, and the unusual solitude was best in tune with the faint hues, the long deep shadows, the fragrant atmosphere. In the trees of the street the sparrows were chattering merrily before going to roost, and from the church a single drowsy bell was summoning the faithful to a week-day's evening service. The clocks in the house ticked softly one against another, and the apartment wore that mournful and expectant air which places, usually full of voices and movement, assume when they are deserted by their familiar crowds, the flowers shedding their perfume on the empty air, and the grand pianoforte standing mute with its shut music-scores lying on its ebony case.

'I am so glad to be alone,' she thought, 'and yet——' and yet a sense of loneliness and weariness weighed upon her.

Of Beaufront she had heard nothing for months; she only knew, as all the world knew, that he was out of England with his yacht. She was glad that she had been strong enough to continue firm in the rejection of his suit; she was glad that weakness and selfishness had not made her blind to his interests, and that she had persisted to the end in standing between him and a sacrifice which he would have lived bitterly to repent; but it was a gladness which left her heart heavy and her life dull. She had all that the world could give her in material successes and in the pleasures of the world; but she missed him more and more with every day that passed, and a great sense of heaviness and dejection came over her continually, and she told herself sometimes sadly that she was growing old.

As she sat now in the darkening twilight of the chilly summer eve, with the dreary sound of the single church-bell alone jarring on the stillness, she thought of the days of her childhood in the isles of those far-away warm West Indian seas; of the many chimes of St. Pierre swinging melodiously over the city, of the black robes of the nuns and the white robes of the choristers, and the many-coloured banners swaying under the deep blue sky, and the negro children running with the pyramids of gorgeous blossom, and the light laughing everywhere on the sparkling waves, and the crowded streets and the gorgeous fruits and the golden rays of the upraised Host.

'I will go back there and end my days,' she thought. 'I have had enough of this world. I know it in all its fairness and in all its rottenness. I will enter some convent and spend my money amongst the poor.

>Et mourir ne doit être rien,
>Puisque vivre est si peu de chose!'

There was a chair opposite to her; a long, low, lounging chair covered with silk embroidered by herself. It was the favourite chair of her lost friend, and he had occupied it scores of times, hundreds of times, sitting there opposite to her with his colley dog at his feet. She saw the vacant seat now through a mist of tears which started to her eyes but did not fall. Is living so slight a thing? she thought; sometimes it was pain enough, and sometimes it would seem as though it would never end.

Her servant roused her from her melancholy meditations as he crossed the room and murmured very diffidently in fear of having disobeyed her orders.

'Lady Avillion asks if you receive, Madam. I thought perhaps you would wish to make an exception for her.'

She looked up with intense surprise and vague emotion.

'Lady Avillion!' she repeated with incredulity. 'Here? Of course I am at home to her.'

In her intense amazement at such a visit, she had but one thought; it must augur some misfortune, some accident, some danger to Beaufront. Could less than death itself bring into her presence the one person who alone of all the great world of London had refused for eight years to cross the threshold of her house?

She stood in the middle of the room, motionless, bloodless, her heart beating to suffocation, her mind thronged with images of his possible suffering, of his possible peril. And yet why, even for sake of his death itself, should this cold, disdainful, and exclusive woman come to the house which she had avoided for so long, as though it were a lazar-house?

In another moment Lady Avillion had entered the room. She held out her hand with the gesture of a friend. She smiled slightly; the smile was pale and fleeting, but it was kind.

'I am come—' she said simply, 'I am come to beg your pardon.'

Consuelo Laurence gazed blankly at her. She did not take her hand nor did she give her any greeting.

'There is no misfortune then? No accident to Ralph?' she said in a hushed and broken voice, whilst the blood rushed back through her veins and coloured her delicate cheeks. She could scarcely speak for the beating of her heart.

Freda smiled again; that brief, slight, passing smile which had no life or light in it, and yet had an infinite compassion.

'Do you care so much as that?'

Absorbed as Consuelo Laurence was in her own emotions, she was startled by the change which she saw in the features of her visitant. It was a change nameless, impalpable, intangible, but as great as the change from midsummer to winter in a landscape. All her beautiful colouring was gone, and her eyes had a strained, sleepless, sightless look in them painful to behold. There was no actual physical alteration, yet nothing was as it had been in her. Her proud and stately carriage was the same, and she had no physical sign of age or illness, or even of pain, and yet all youth had gone for ever out of her. Still young in years, she was for ever old.

She said again, with a weary sort of wonder in her voice,

'Do you care so much as that?'

Consuelo did not speak; her breath came and went rapidly, she asked no other questions, nothing else seemed to her to matter.

The servant was moving here and there, placing the various lamps; Freda waited till he had left the room, then she said once more:

'I have come to beg your pardon.'

'There is no need for that,' replied Consuelo Laurence with gentle coldness; 'you have always had full right to your opinions, if they did me wrong.'

'And I have also come to ask you to be my cousin's wife.'

She spoke without warmth, mechanically, like one who recites a lesson; she did what she wished to do, what she knew it was right to do, but she could not force her heart into the act, for it seemed to her that her heart was dead.

Consuelo Laurence gazed at her in utter and blank amazement. She doubted her own senses. She still said nothing; she still saw the face and form of her visitant as in a mist, and she still doubted her own hearing.

'My cousin came home yesterday,' continued Lady Avillion. 'I saw him this morning. I am certain that his happiness lies with you, and you alone. I know that you have repeatedly refused him, because you have considered that such a marriage would be adverse to his interests and unfit for his position. I do not disguise from you that I did my utmost to dissuade him from it. I have done you harm in English society and I am sorry that I did so. I have become convinced that his heart is set on making you his wife, and I know that you care for him, for he showed me the letter of refusal which you wrote to him in the autumn, and it was the letter of a very noble woman, and of a woman who loved another better than herself. He thinks that if I ask you to marry him, you will do so. Will you? I will do my best to repair the evil I have done, and if you will become his wife you shall become also my most esteemed friend. What I say my family will say after me. You can refuse no longer now.'

'Give me time—let me think—you cannot be serious,' said Consuelo Laurence, with an agitation which she could not control, and an incredulity which she could not conquer, as she gazed vacantly at one who had been her enemy so many years, and now came to her as an angel of peace and of light.

'I am serious, and I speak in all seriousness. I believe in you as Beaufront believes in you; and as I know that the happiness of his future is in your hands I beg you not to trifle with it for any mere punctilio, or apprehension, or want of faith in yourself or in him. I have been an arrogant, foolish, narrow egotist. I have misjudged the meanings and the values of human life. It is too late for me to change. I shall live my life out with my false gods. But you—you have a living man's heart in your hands. Keep it close to yours, and be happy while you can.'

Then, before the other could speak, she touched the cheek of Consuelo Laurence with her lips in sign of perpetual amity and future kinship.

'I will send Ralph to you,' she said softly; and then she went away into the twilight of the streets; alone with her dead love, with her empty heart, with her false gods, alone for ever in the midst of the gay great world.

THE END.

www.ingramcontent.com/pod-product-compliance
Lightning Source LLC
Chambersburg PA
CBHW020235240426
43672CB00006B/530